I0414295

ENFORCEMENT IS NOT OPTIONAL: THE GOLDMAN ACT TO RETURN ABDUCTED AMERICAN CHILDREN

HEARING

BEFORE THE

SUBCOMMITTEE ON AFRICA, GLOBAL HEALTH, GLOBAL HUMAN RIGHTS, AND INTERNATIONAL ORGANIZATIONS

OF THE

COMMITTEE ON FOREIGN AFFAIRS HOUSE OF REPRESENTATIVES

ONE HUNDRED FIFTEENTH CONGRESS

FIRST SESSION

APRIL 6, 2017

Serial No. 115–17

Printed for the use of the Committee on Foreign Affairs

Available via the World Wide Web: http://www.foreignaffairs.house.gov/ or
http://www.gpo.gov/fdsys/

U.S. GOVERNMENT PUBLISHING OFFICE

24–918PDF   WASHINGTON : 2017

For sale by the Superintendent of Documents, U.S. Government Publishing Office
Internet: bookstore.gpo.gov   Phone: toll free (866) 512–1800; DC area (202) 512–1800
Fax: (202) 512–2104   Mail: Stop IDCC, Washington, DC 20402–0001

COMMITTEE ON FOREIGN AFFAIRS

EDWARD R. ROYCE, California, *Chairman*

CHRISTOPHER H. SMITH, New Jersey
ILEANA ROS-LEHTINEN, Florida
DANA ROHRABACHER, California
STEVE CHABOT, Ohio
JOE WILSON, South Carolina
MICHAEL T. McCAUL, Texas
TED POE, Texas
DARRELL E. ISSA, California
TOM MARINO, Pennsylvania
JEFF DUNCAN, South Carolina
MO BROOKS, Alabama
PAUL COOK, California
SCOTT PERRY, Pennsylvania
RON DeSANTIS, Florida
MARK MEADOWS, North Carolina
TED S. YOHO, Florida
ADAM KINZINGER, Illinois
LEE M. ZELDIN, New York
DANIEL M. DONOVAN, JR., New York
F. JAMES SENSENBRENNER, JR.,
  Wisconsin
ANN WAGNER, Missouri
BRIAN J. MAST, Florida
FRANCIS ROONEY, Florida
BRIAN K. FITZPATRICK, Pennsylvania
THOMAS A. GARRETT, JR., Virginia

ELIOT L. ENGEL, New York
BRAD SHERMAN, California
GREGORY W. MEEKS, New York
ALBIO SIRES, New Jersey
GERALD E. CONNOLLY, Virginia
THEODORE E. DEUTCH, Florida
KAREN BASS, California
WILLIAM R. KEATING, Massachusetts
DAVID N. CICILLINE, Rhode Island
AMI BERA, California
LOIS FRANKEL, Florida
TULSI GABBARD, Hawaii
JOAQUIN CASTRO, Texas
ROBIN L. KELLY, Illinois
BRENDAN F. BOYLE, Pennsylvania
DINA TITUS, Nevada
NORMA J. TORRES, California
BRADLEY SCOTT SCHNEIDER, Illinois
THOMAS R. SUOZZI, New York
ADRIANO ESPAILLAT, New York
TED LIEU, California

AMY PORTER, *Chief of Staff*   THOMAS SHEEHY, *Staff Director*

JASON STEINBAUM, *Democratic Staff Director*

SUBCOMMITTEE ON AFRICA, GLOBAL HEALTH, GLOBAL HUMAN RIGHTS, AND INTERNATIONAL ORGANIZATIONS

CHRISTOPHER H. SMITH, New Jersey, *Chairman*

MARK MEADOWS, North Carolina
DANIEL M. DONOVAN, JR., New York
F. JAMES SENSENBRENNER, JR.,
  Wisconsin
THOMAS A. GARRETT, JR., Virginia

KAREN BASS, California
AMI BERA, California
JOAQUIN CASTRO, Texas
THOMAS R. SUOZZI, New York

CONTENTS

ENFORCEMENT IS NOT OPTIONAL: THE GOLDMAN ACT TO RETURN ABDUCTED AMERICAN CHILDREN

THURSDAY, APRIL 6, 2017

House of Representatives,
Subcommittee on Africa, Global Health,
Global Human Rights, and International Organizations,
Committee on Foreign Affairs,
Washington, DC.

The subcommittee met, pursuant to notice, at 10:00 a.m., in room 2172, Rayburn House Office Building, Hon. Christopher H. Smith (chairman of the subcommittee) presiding.

Mr. SMITH. The subcommittee will come to order, and good afternoon to everyone. I want to thank all of you, especially all of the left-behind parents I see in the audience, for joining us this after- noon to discuss the continuing crisis of international parental child abduction.

Today there is hope that the new administration will change the status quo. There is hope that the Sean and David Goldman International Child Abduction Prevention and Return Act will finally be enforced and there is hope for those of you who seek to be reunited with your children that a better day is coming.

As many of you here today have experienced, international parental child abduction rips children from their homes and whisks them away to a foreign land, alienating them from the love and care of the parent and family that is left behind.

Child abduction is child abuse and continues to plague families across the United States. According to the State Department's statistics, approximately 1,000 children are today held hostage in a foreign country, separated from their American parent. Several hundred additional children join their ranks every year.

Based on historical trends, less than a third of these children will ever come home, unless, of course, the Trump administration decides to do what the previous administration did not do: Change tack and stand up for the American parents and children using the full—I repeat full—array of tools prescribed by the Goldman Act to help achieve the necessary objective.

I was heartened to hear that many of you visited the White House this morning. This is a good sign and gives rise to the expectation that your voices will be heard. Indeed, I join you in imploring President Donald Trump to act and to act decisively.

(1)

For decades and throughout the Obama administration, the State Department has used quiet diplomacy to attempt to bring these children home. In a hearing that I chaired back in 2009, former Assistant Secretary of State Bernie Aronson called quiet diplomacy, and I quote him, "a sophisticated form of begging." Thousands of American families are still ruptured and grieving from years of unresolved abductions, confirming that quiet diplomacy alone is gravely inadequate.

In 2014, after 5 years of persistence, Congress unanimously passed the Goldman Act to give teeth to requests for return and access. The actions against noncooperating governments required by the law escalate in gravity and range from official protests through diplomatic channels, to the suspension of development, security, or other foreign assistance. Extradition of abducting parents also may be called for.

The Goldman Act is a law designed to get results, as we did with the return of Sean Goldman from Brazil in 2009. Brazil's participation in the Generalized System of Preferences is up again for renewal this year. Why should Brazil get billions of dollars in tariff relief when their courts have not returned a single child since Sean Goldman? We have 13 long-term cases pending there, including the particularly egregious Brann and Davenport cases. It is time for action and fully taking advantage of our leverage.

More than 90 American children are separated from their American parent in India. The many years required to resolve such cases in India make it a magnet for abduction cases and crimes. These numbers will continue to climb each year until India creates a mechanism for resolution of current cases or joins the Hague Convention for future cases, which to date it has refused to do.

Thinking outside the box as to what leverage to apply, India's visa allotment could be reduced every year if it is noncompliant in the return of abducted American children. But there are many, many options on the table and, again, so many that were prescribed by the Goldman Act.

Japan is another country which is a flagrant violator. American servicemembers, whose lives are on the line protecting Japan, are some of the victims.

The Obama administration's indefensible refusal to use the sanctioning tools embedded in the Goldman Act has been noted by other governments and is hurting American children. On February 14, for example, Valentine's Day, Japan's Minister of Foreign Affairs, Fumio Kishida, noted that in their Parliament, the Diet, and I quote him, "Until now, there is not a single example in which the U.S. applied Goldman Act sanctions toward foreign countries."

Let me repeat that. Until now, the Foreign Minister has said, there is not a single example in which the United States, U.S., applied sanctions, Goldman Act sanctions, toward foreign countries. That is outrageous and that has to change.

Three days later, the Osaka High Court overturned a return order for four American children to James Cook, who will testify today, in flagrant violation of the Hague Convention, Japan's own Hague implementation guide, and United States law. Japan fears no consequence—had no fear of consequence under the Obama administration—and thus are children are left behind and their parents suffer the pain of separation.

The Elias family is here today. They have been waiting 8 years to even speak with their children after a flagrant abduction in which the Japanese Consulate was an accessory. I traveled to Japan with the grandmother, and I can tell you, she tried, as has Michael, over and over and over again to even have access to his kids. And, again, there has been a closed-door policy.

We need to apply the Goldman Act sanctions to Japan. Yes, they are a friend and an ally. All the more reason. Friends don't let friends commit human rights abuses.

Dr. Frisancho, who is one of our witnesses today, has been waiting 7 years for Slovakia to enforce the return for his children. As a matter of fact, he says in his testimony: Is enforcement of U.S. law optional? Why is it that we have not had the full, all-out enforcement of the United States law under the Obama administration? I hope and I pray, and we will press, that the new administration will not continue that pattern of indifference.

When is enough enough? What we need is a change in the culture of the State Department, which too often rewards Foreign Service Officers for appeasing countries in the name of maintaining harmonious relations. And, frankly, I have been on this committee for 35 years, in Congress now 37, and I can tell you, I travel. We have very fine people who serve as Foreign Service Officers. But when you rock the boat, when you stand up for Americans, that is not a career enhancement process for you. That has to change. So the culture of the Department of State has to change.

Implementing the Goldman Act fully and robustly will send a message to allies and foes alike that the United States means business about ending the suffering of American families and we mean business when it comes to these children.

Dr. Hunter, I saw, and she will lead off our testimony today, in her opening paragraphs makes a just very, very profound statement, "This Congress and this administration represents our best opportunity ever to put America first for America's stolen children, and make the return of American children to the United States a priority again."

I want to thank her and all of our witnesses for your testimonies.

Without objection, they all in their fullness and any additional information you would like to add will be made a part of the record.

We are joined by my good friend and colleague, Mr. Garrett. Would you like to——

Mr. GARRETT. Briefly, Mr. Chairman, I just want to thank you and recognize you for your 35-year commitment to causes such as this in this body. I tell people oftentimes, Mr. Chairman, that sometimes you find your passion and sometimes your passion finds you. It has been my great honor for just these few months to serve on this subcommittee with you.

And these are issues that all too often are unheard by the American public, and it is something that we sort of, as you know, dove headlong into. And it is just an honor to be able to work with you for such a great cause and with people such as yourselves.

Please, I welcome anyone in the gallery to contact our office as it relates to concerns that you may have so that we can leverage whatever little power we have to yield to help to have the return of our children to their families in our Nation, and thank you.

And I yield back the remainder of my time.

Mr. SMITH. Mr. Garrett, thank you very much. And thank you for your service to our country in the Armed Services, but also for stepping up on a variety of human rights issues so early in your tenure as a Member of Congress.

I would like to now introduce our distinguished panel, beginning first with Dr. Noelle Hunter, who is the executive director of the Kentucky Office of Highway Safety and has been in that role since June 2016.

In 2014, Dr. Hunter testified before the U.S. Senate Committee on Foreign Relations on the problem of international parental child abduction. She successfully recovered her daughter from abduction to Mali that same year with the support and resources from her home community of Morehead, her native State of Alabama, and from Congress, the U.S. Department of State, and the U.S. Department of Justice.

She co-founded iStand Parent Network to empower parents to return their children from abduction and currently serves as president of the board of directors.

Thank you, Doctor, for being here.

I then will turn to Mr. James Cook, who is the father of four children, two sets of twins, who were abducted and are now in Japan. In this time he has only been allowed one visit with his children and has not been allowed any access to them since August 2015.

Mr. Cook works for Boston Scientific Corporation, a manufacturer of medical devices in Minnesota. Mr. Cook testified before this subcommittee in July of last year and again we welcome him back and look forward to updates and insights that he can provide.

We will then hear from Dr. Augusto Frisancho, father of children abducted to Slovakia. He is a physician and received his medical degree in general medicine from Charles University in Prague in the Czech Republic. He works at Johns Hopkins University in Baltimore, in public health medical research. He also works for the National Center for Missing and Exploited Children as a consultant, providing support to families impacted by a missing child. His three children were abducted to Slovakia by his wife in 2010.

Then we will hear from Mr. Vikram Jagtiani, whose daughter Nikhita was born in New York, taken by his wife in 2013 when she was just 4 years old. Wanting to see his daughter again, he co-founded Bring Our Kids Home, along with other left-behind parents whose children have been abducted to India from the United States. Bring Our Kids Home seeks to raise awareness about international parental child abductions community and advocates for the prompt return of all American children.

Dr. Hunter, the floor is yours.

STATEMENT OF NOELLE HUNTER, PH.D., FOUNDER, ISTAND PARENT NETWORK (MOTHER OF CHILD RETURNED FROM MALI)

Ms. HUNTER. Good morning. Thank you, Mr. Chairman, thank you, Mr. Garrett, for taking the opportunity to attend today.

We have just recently come from the White House, myself and my fellow parents. It was a very productive meeting. We were very candid about the concerns that we have about current enforcement of the Goldman Act. But more importantly, there is an opportunity here to put America first for America's stolen children.

I am honored to share my story and speak for fellow parents of internationally abducted children. As you said, sir, this Congress and this administration represent our best opportunity ever to put America first for America's stolen children and make the return of America's kidnapped children a priority to the United States.

I am president and co-founder of iStand Parent Network. My daughter, Muna, was a victim of international parental child abduction. She was abducted from our home in Morehead, Kentucky, on December 27, 2011—she was only 4 years old at the time—and taken to Mali, west Africa, by her father.

Despite some initial delays, I soon had court orders for her return and cases with the FBI, the Department of State's Office of Children's Issues, and the National Center for Missing and Exploited Children. My experience with all of these agencies was exceptional, responsive, and accomplished the goal.

Sadly, this is not most parents' experience. Most parents find the return of their children is subordinated to not making nations feel uncomfortable.

Mali initially showed no interest in working with me or our Government to return Muna. That all changed in November 2012, the day I staged a protest in front of the Mali Embassy here in Washington and subsequently engaged my congressional delegation, including Senate Majority Leader Mitch McConnell, Senator Rand Paul, and Chairman Hal Rogers.

I am grateful that Muna's case became very personal for Senator McConnell and Chairman Rogers in particular. They constantly engaged with the Department of State, Department of Justice, and Malian officials in Washington and Bamako. Chairman Rogers raised our case directly with former Secretary of State John Kerry during an Appropriations hearing. Senator McConnell progressively escalated his interactions with the nation of Mali while receiving regular updates from the State Department.

I was blessed to have benefited from a whole-of-government response, and that is the reason that Muna is home today.

Just before she came home, as you said, sir, Senator Corker invited me to testify on the Goldman Act, legislation that was supposed to make life easier for parents who are trying to return their children, before the Senate Committee on Foreign Relations. And, of course, Mr. Chairman, you have been our champion all along, drafting and shepherding the Goldman Act until its eventual enactment. And I believe I speak for all of the parents when I say that we thank you. You give us hope that our children can come home. This is all the momentum that I took with me to Mali in the summer of 2014. U.S. Ambassador Mary Beth Leonard and con-sular officers facilitated a meeting with Mali's Minister of Justice, and that day I knew that I was coming home with my daughter. We were escorted out of the country by United States Marines, and Ambassador Leonard herself put us on the airplane. When we arrived at Cincinnati/Northern Kentucky International Airport, my beloved Senator McConnell was there to welcome us home.

I am told that my story is unique, and, sir, this is tragic. It should not be this way. If every Member of Congress with kidnapped constituents would begin to regularly inquire of Federal agencies and the nations in which they are held and also require enforcement of the Goldman Act and other laws that are designed to make it easier to bring our children home, we would see an immediate surge in returns and reunifications of children with their parents.

A whole-of-government support of parents who have had their children stolen from them would also create a very strong deterrent for would-be abductors and put nations on notice that America will not tolerate the theft of its children.

There are a few things, sir, that need to happen to hasten those outcomes and make my story less unique. The Trump administration has a golden opportunity to show parents across these United States whose children have been kidnapped to countries that actively work against their return that it supports these parents and will do all it can to bring our children home.

As I said, I was blessed to have the active involvement of the Kentucky congressional delegation, the Department of State, and the Department of Justice, including in the Department of State Ambassador Leonard and Embassy staff in Bamako. But every taxpaying parent, every single one in the United States, deserves the full-throated, aggressive support of our Government.

The Trump administration has a chance to signal its intent to support American parents where prior administrations have failed to do so. "America First" must mean putting America's stolen children first.

Countries around the world that are harboring American children and ignoring their legal obligations need to be put on notice that it is time to comply. The worst offenders in the international community, countries like Brazil, India, and Japan, need to be more forcefully addressed and not given a pass by diplomats. Laws need to be taken seriously and enforced, and there need to be consequences for failing to adhere to international obligations and other commitments. And in circumstances where countries still refuse to return our children, they should no longer receive the benefits from the United States, such as favorable trade agreements, visas, and foreign aid, until they do comply.

Case in point, Brazil, as you mentioned earlier, has aided and abetted the kidnapping of many American citizen children, but the United States Government has to date failed to take this issue seriously, and Brazil has responded accordingly. If Brazil does not start returning children to the United States quickly and make other good faith efforts to show that it intends to return all American children, the United States has an opportunity later this year, in 2017, to deny Brazil the over $2 billion benefit it receives by taking part in the United States Generalized System of Preferences, or GSP. Brazil must literally pay a price for noncompliance here, and the GSP represents a perfect opportunity to demonstrate seriousness.

Similarly, India has aggressively refused to return American children, but the President has the authority to prevent H-1B visas and other lucrative work visas from being issued to an India national if it does not start returning American children. India, too, can be forced to pay a price.

The Department of State must prioritize the return of American children over diplomatic niceties. It is understandable that diplomats believe in success through dialogue, but when it comes to international parental child abduction, let's be clear: The goal is not dialogue, but the return of abducted children, period. The Department of State needs to be refocused on what is most important: Putting America's children first. Dialogue is a means to an end and not an end itself.

Transparency with the Congress and the American people is essential. The Department of State definitively has the capability to report specific data to Congress to inform your casework, legislation, and oversight. It has the data collection and analytical tools necessary to report abductions by state and plot abductor destination countries on a world map.

Despite this capacity, the Department of State has, respectfully, made a concerted effort to keep the scope of this problem hidden, particularly during the previous administration, and it did so for one very important reason: It was terrified that Congress might not only have a fuller understanding of the scope of this problem, but that it, Congress, might also have more tools to bring many of these children home. The State Department can improve its forthcoming report by drilling down on this data and making it publicly available.

Federal laws, both civil and criminal, must be enforced. Enforcement of the Goldman Act and other Federal laws that are supposed to help parents is the way forward. It directs progressive sanctions against worst offender nations who benefit from economic, cultural, and diplomatic relationships with the United States and yet refuse to return our children, hold them captive.

The Department of State need to stop issuing demarches, diplomatic wrist slaps behind closed doors, and start using the full array of tools outlined in the Goldman Act, including sanctions against noncompliant countries, in order to be most effective.

The Department of Justice has options that can and should be considered as well. While many abducting parents do not generally leave the country where they have taken their abducted children, some do. In fact, some own property and assets internationally, including in the United States, and even travel for business, sometimes frequently. Each of these international assets and points of travel is a point of leverage for abducting parents and should be actively explored.

International agreements governing international child abductions must also be enforced. The Hague Convention on the Civil Aspects of International Child Abduction, which is the governing treaty for international parental child abductions, does work for some, and we are aware of a handful of cases, comparatively speaking, of children who have come home by this process. In fact, I just learned of a parent whose son was abducted to Italy who recently came through a Hague return order.

We are very happy any time a parent and child are reunited for whom this process is working. But they are, I am, in a minority of successful cases. The aforementioned nations and other state parties which acceded to the Hague Convention and yet decline to enforce access or return of children to their habitual residence in the United States under that convention must be held accountable. Finally, there must be a persistent whole-of-government ap- proach to bring children home. For nations like Mali, which is not a signatory to the Hague Abduction Convention, there must be pressure and insistence on returns. Though it was never said to me, sir, I am quite certain that Mali was becoming distinctively un- comfortable with the level of attention by me, Muna's supporters, and my Government, the United States Government, which would not let my daughter be lost.

I am confident that other nations would follow suit as Mali to let these children go should they come under greater scrutiny. We can see the result in every country that is harboring abducted children if every Presidential trip, every diplomatic delegation, every con- gressional delegation raises the crisis of our children when visiting these countries. More children will come home once these countries understand that we are not going away and we will not forget our children.

What matters most is that we stand united for their return, for Hannah and Ryan, Eslam and Zander, Mochi and Keisuke, Reyansh, Roshni and Rachel, Eliav and Abdallah, Gabriel and Anastasia, Henry and Helena, and all of America's stolen children.

May we not rest, may this country not rest, until the banner of liberty and freedom that we enshrine and believe in is extended over them to usher them home.

Thank you, sir.

[The prepared statement of Ms. Hunter follows:]

Noelle Hunter, Ph.D.
Mother of Returned Child
President & Co-Founder
iStand Parent Network Inc.
U.S. House Committee on Foreign Affairs
Subcommittee on Africa, Global Health, Global Human Rights, and International
Organizations
April 6, 2017, Enforcement is Not Optional: The Goldman Act to Return Abducted
American Children

Thank you Mr. Chairman and Mr. Vice Chairman. I'm an honored to share my story and
speak for my fellow parents of internationally-abducted children. This Congress and this
Administration represents our best opportunity ever to put America First for America's
Stolen Children, and make the return of American children to the United States a priority
again.

I'm president and co-founder of iStand Parent Network. My daughter, Muna, was a
victim of International Parental Child Abduction, when she was kidnapped by her father
to Mali, West Africa, in 2011. She was only four years old. Despite some initial delays, I
soon had court orders for her return, and cases with the FBI, the Department of State's
Office of Children's Issues, and the National Center for Missing and Exploited
Children. My experiences with all of these agencies was exceptional, responsive and
accomplished the goal. Unfortunately, this is not most parents' experience, since most
parents find that the return of their children is subordinated to not making the
international community uncomfortable.

Mali initially showed no interest in working with me and our government to return
Muna. That changed in November 2012, the day I staged a protest in front of the Mali
Embassy here in Washington and subsequently engaged my congressional delegation,
which includes Majority Leader Mitch McConnell, Senator Rand Paul, and Chairman
Harold Rogers.

I am grateful that Muna's case became very personal to Chairman Rogers and Senator
McConnell in particular, and they consistently engaged with the Departments of State
and Justice and Malian officials in Washington and Bamako. Representatives of that
nation were called to the Hill to give account for why this American child remained
separated from her mother, sisters, and family. Chairman Rogers raised our case
directly with former Secretary of State John Kerry during an appropriations hearing.
Senator McConnell progressively escalated his interactions with Mali while receiving
regular updates from the State Department. I was blessed to have benefited from a
whole-of-government response, which is the only reason why Muna is home today.

Just before Muna came home, Senator Corker invited me to testify on the Goldman Act,
which was legislation that was supposed to make it easier for parents like myself, before
the Senate Committee on Foreign Relations. And, of course, Mr. Chairman, you were

our champion all along, shepherding the Goldman Act to its eventually enactment. All of this momentum I carried with me to Mali in summer 2014.

U.S. Ambassador Mary Beth Leonard and consular officers facilitated a meeting with Mali's Minister of Justice, and that day, I knew we were coming home. We were escorted out of the country by U.S. Marines and put on the airplane by Ambassador Leonard herself. When we arrived at Northern Kentucky airport, my dear senator was there to welcome us home.

I'm told my story is unique, which is tragic. It doesn't have to be. If every member of Congress with kidnapped constituents would begin to regularly inquire of federal agencies and nations in which they are held, and also require enforcement of the Goldman Act and other laws that were designed to make it easier to bring our children home, we would see an immediate surge in returns and reunifications of children with their parents. Whole-of-government support of parents who have had their children stolen from them would also create a strong deterrent for would-be abductors and put nations on notice that America will not tolerate the theft of its children.

There are few things that need to happen to hasten these outcomes, and make my story less unique.

The Trump Administration has a golden opportunity to show the parents across the United States, whose children have been kidnapped to countries that actively work against the return of their children, that it supports these parents, and will do all it can to bring their children home. As I said, I was blessed to have the active involvement of the Kentucky congressional delegation, the Department of Justice, and the Department of State, which includes Ambassador Leonard and embassy staff in Bamako. But every taxpaying parent in the United States deserves the full-throated, aggressive support of their government. The Trump Administration has a chance to signal this intent to support American parents where prior administrations refused to do so.

Countries around the world that are harboring American children, and ignoring their legal obligations, need to be put on notice that it is time to comply. The worst offenders in the international community – countries like Brazil, India, and Japan – need to be more forcefully addressed, and not given a pass by diplomats. Laws need to be taken seriously and enforced, and there need to be consequences for failing to adhere to international obligations and other commitments. And in circumstances where countries still refuse to return our children, they should no longer receive benefits from the United States, such as favorable trade treatment, visas, and foreign aid, until they do comply.

Case in point: Brazil's government has aided and abetted the kidnapping of many American citizen children, but the United States government has, to date, failed to take the issue seriously, and Brazil has acted accordingly. If Brazil does not start returning children to the United States quickly, and make other good faith efforts to show that it intends to return all American children, the United States has an opportunity later this year, in 2017, to deny Brazil the $2 billion benefit it receives by taking part in the United States' Generalized System of Preferences, or GSP. Brazil must literally pay a price for noncompliance here, and the GSP represents a perfect opportunity to demonstrate seriousness.

Similarly, India has aggressively refused to return American children, but the President has the authority to prevent H-1B visas and other lucrative work visas from being issued to Indian nationals if it does not start returning American children. India, too, can be forced to pay a price.

The Department of State must prioritize the return of American children over diplomatic niceties. It is understandable that diplomats believe in success through dialogue. But when it comes to international parental child abduction, let's be clear: the goal is not dialogue, but the return of abducted American children. Period. The Department of State needs to be refocused on what is most important. Dialogue is a means to an end, not an end in itself.

Transparency, with Congress and the American people, is essential. The Department of State definitively has the capability to report specific data to Congress to inform your casework, legislation and oversight. It has the data collection and analytical tools necessary to report abductions by state, and plot abductor destination countries on a world map. Despite this capacity, the Department of State has, respectfully, made a concerted effort to keep the scope of the problem hidden, particularly during the previous administration, and it did so for one very important reason: it was terrified that Congress might have not only a fuller understanding of the scope of the problem, but also that it – meaning Congress – had the tools to bring many of these kids home. It can improve its forthcoming report by drilling down on this data and making it publicly available.

Federal law, both civil and criminal, must be enforced. Enforcement of the Goldman Act, and other federal laws that are supposed to help parents, is the way forward. It directs progressive sanctions against worst offender nations who benefit from economic, cultural and diplomatic relationships with the United States and yet hold our children captive. The Department of State needs to stop using demarches – which are diplomatic wrist-slaps behind closed doors – and start using the full array of tools authorized by the Goldman Act, including sanctions against non-compliant countries, in order to be most effective.

And the Department of Justice has options that can and should be considered. While many abducting parents do not generally leave the country where they have taken their abducted children, some do. In fact, some own property and assets internationally, including in the United States, and even travel internationally for business, sometimes frequently. Each of these international assets or occasions of travel is a point of leverage against abducting parents, and should be actively explored.

International agreements governing international parental child abductions must also be enforced. The Hague Convention on the Civil Aspects of International Child Abduction, which is the governing treaty for international parental child abductions, does work for some, and we are aware of a handful of cases, comparatively speaking, of children who have come home by this process. I just learned of a parent whose son was abducted to Italy who recently came home through a Hague return order.

We are so happy for the parents and children for whom this process works. But they are, I am, a minority of successful cases. The aforementioned nations and other states parties which acceded to the Hague and yet decline to enforce access or return children to their habitual residence in the U.S. under that convention must be held accountable.

There must be a persistent, whole-of-government effort to bring children home. For nations like Mali, which is not a signatory to the Hague Abduction Convention, there must also be pressure and insistence on returns. Though it was never said to me, I got the distinct impression that Mali was growing increasingly uncomfortable with pressure from me and Muna's supporters and under the intent gaze of the United States government, which would not let my daughter be lost. I am confident that other nations would swiftly follow Mali's suit and let these children go, should they come under greater scrutiny. We can see results in every country that is harboring abducted American children if every presidential trip, every diplomatic delegation, and every congressional delegation raises the issue of these children when they visit these countries. More children will come home once these countries understand that we are not going away, and will not forget.

Mechanisms built into Section 202 of the Goldman Act direct specific actions against countries determined to have a pattern of noncompliance. We've had demarches and official public statements. It's time now to use those other actions:

- public condemnation;
- a delay or cancellation of one or more bilateral working, official, or state visits;
- the withdrawal, limitation, or suspension of U.S. development or security assistance, or assistance to a central government;
- a formal request to a foreign country to extradite an individual who is engaged in abduction and who has been formally accused of, charged with, or convicted of an extraditable offense; or
- other commensurate actions.

Additionally, on behalf of the Coalition to End International Parental Child Abduction, we offer the following recommendations:

Discontinue certain visa categories for the foreign nationals of non-compliant or non-cooperating countries. The United States should discontinue pending and new visa applications from certain visa categories for citizens or foreign nationals seeking admission to the United States for countries that demonstrate patterns of non-compliance or non-cooperation in returning abducted American children.

Issue travel alerts. The State Department should issue travel alerts on its website warning Americans about the dangers of child abductions to countries that demonstrate patterns of non-compliance or non-cooperation in returning abducted American children.

Negotiate return MOUs and bilateral agreements. For non-signatory nations like India and Tunisia the U.S. should bilateral agreements, memorandums of understanding, and other tools that explicitly outline processes for resolving abductions and returning children home and also contain explicit penalties for noncompliance as stipulated in the Goldman Act.

Expedite return applications. Expedite the filing of return applications with Central Authority/Administrative Agency in destination Country, for all American children whose child abduction case has been reported to State Department

Simplify prevention. Prevention initiatives have expanded and robust conversations have yielded some success. The Prevent Abduction Program needs to be simplified and publicly available.

Amend definitions in the Goldman Act. Amend definitions in the Goldman Act to define a case as one child; include access cases in abduction case counts; amend the definition of "child" (to avoid age outs); amend the definitions of resolved and unresolved cases; redefine report categories so that all abducted children are counted.

Improve communications and engagement with the IPCA parent-stakeholder community. Parent input is vital to reforming this issue and In fact, the Interagency Task Force established by the Goldman Act would be greatly enhanced by input and participation by representatives from the parent community.

Raise the public profile of IPCA. Congress can engage multiple constituencies around IPCA about the sheer numbers of American children who have been taken from this nation. More than 1000 U.S. children are abducted by a parent annually. That's 5000 children taken from the U.S. from 2010-1013. Based on those statistics, 29,000 American children have been abducted since the Office of Children's Issues was established. That is the size of a small town. Gone.

Fund research on IPCA. Congress should fund an independent agency to research and update the literature on IPCA in the U.S. We are recycling numbers from federal-funded publications from as far back as 1999.

I thank you for this opportunity to share our story and to make recommendations for your consideration so that Enforcement of the Goldman Act is non-optional. This has been an extraordinary day for us, full hope for what can happen when we put America's children first.

What matters most is that we stand united for their return, for Hannah and Ryan, Eslam and Zander, Mochi and Keisuke, Reyansh, Roshni and Rachel, Eliav and Abdallah, Gabriel and Anastasia and all of America's Stolen Children - may we not rest until the banner of liberty and freedom that enshrine and believe in, is extended over them to usher them home.

Thank you.

———————

Mr. Smith. Dr. Hunter, thank you so very much for your testimony and for laying out a number of very, very important ways forward. Thank you.

Ms. Hunter. Thank you.

Mr. Smith. Mr. Cook.

STATEMENT OF MR. JAMES COOK (FATHER OF CHILDREN ABDUCTED TO JAPAN)

Mr. Cook. Thank you, Chairman Smith, members of the subcommittee, and members of the audience watching these proceedings all over the world. I really appreciate this opportunity to speak to you a second time about my Hague Convention case in Japan and the problems encountered following the previous testimony given last July.

First, I want to say hello to my children, because I have not been allowed any access to them since August 2015. This is in direct violation of Hague and evidence of Japan's continuing noncompliance. Hello, children. I have not and will not give up having us together again in the USA. I am sorry this situation has not been resolved by now. I am closer than ever before to having us together again. Please hold on. Love, Dad.

There were two failed Hague return enforcement attempts in Nara, Japan, in September 2016. Direct enforcement was done exactly as Japan requires, an almost SWAT-like ambush where they were living. During the direct enforcement, I was only able to hear the voices of my two older sons, and I did not recognize those voices. It was a sobering reminder of how much has been missed. As a parent, to be unable to recognize your own child's voice brings a type of pain that cannot be described but certainly can be felt as a visceral shudder by all parents.

At the direct enforcement attempts, there were court officers, police, psychologists, and officials from the Japanese Central Authority and U.S. Consulate. With the exception of U.S. officials, it was obvious that everyone else was there to protect the children from me trying to see them and to thoroughly document an anticipated, calculated failure. I foolishly thought these officials I had paid to execute direct enforcement were there for my success. In reality, they were just playing their roles of predetermined outcome, failure.

Furthermore, and worst of all, it severely traumatized our children in a way that did not need to happen.

With the unsuccessful enforcement attempts, Japan has once again failed to enforce a Hague return order. This time it was the one issued by the Osaka High Court on January 28, 2016. This indicates a systemic problem that was also reported in the annual Hague Compliance report issued just a few days prior to my last testimony in July 2016.

This is 2 years in a row that Japan has been unable to enforce its Hague return orders. This is a systemic problem and should be concerning for any foreign entity planning to enter into contracts or binding agreements with parties in Japan. It certainly should concern foreign governments regarding allowing any of their children to visit Japan.

16

Assumption of subject matter jurisdiction, in accordance with the Osaka High Court return order dated January 28, 2016, and a mirror return order were issued from Hennepin County Family Court in Minnesota on December 2, 2016; then again on December 13, 2016; and then again on January 24, 2017; and then again on March 24, 2017; and then a very thorough analysis of continued subject matter jurisdiction and return order on April 4, 2017.

Will Japan even respect our court's rulings as we are expected to respect theirs?

I was granted temporary sole custody and our children, and they were ordered released to me on December 17, 2016, at the U.S. Consulate in Osaka for their return to the United States. Our children were never brought to the Consulate on that day, in violation of two Minnesota court orders. Hitomi Arimitsu was in contempt of the Minnesota court orders that mirrored the Hague return order of Japan.

I take a moment here. I must acknowledge the significant efforts and resources that were put forth and put in place for that day by the Department of State. Unfortunately, it did not turn out as we wanted it to, but I thank everyone because a great amount of effort was put forth, and I appreciate that.

After a year of unsuccessful enforcement, on January 5, 2017, Hitomi Arimitsu filed for a modification of the Osaka High Court return order citing "grave risk" standard under Hague. The evidence of grave risk cited was of relative lifestyle change if returned. On February 17, 2017, the Osaka High Court Hague return order of January 28, 2016, was revoked, and at this time our children are not being ordered returned by the Osaka High Court.

The revocation of previous return order indicates invalid interpretation of the Hague Convention and provides further evidence of Japan's failure to comply with its international obligation. Article 28 of the Japanese Hague implementing legislation enables an expanded interpretation of grave risk that gives judges broad leeway, way beyond international precedent and language of the Hague, to deny returns. In this instance, it overturned their own previous ruling and in effect made use of the taking parent's ongoing noncompliance with the Hague return order in Japan and from the habitual residence of the children in Minnesota.

Article 28 is not compliant with the Hague, and it must be ordered changed by fellow Hague signatories.

The February 17, 2017, order was signed by Presiding Judge Toru Matsuda, Judge Yoshinori Tanaka, and Judge Takahiro Hiwada. We have appealed this ruling to the Japan Supreme Court and we received permission on March 29 to have our case heard. According to my attorney, it will likely take up to 1 month for the Supreme Court to receive the file from Osaka High Court. If the February 17 decision is overturned, as we fully expect, it will take an additional 6 to 12 months for a Supreme Court hearing.

The projected timeline far exceeds the expeditious processing of Hague cases as outlined in the convention. My case began in August 2015, and it is still unresolved. Japan in yet another way is not compliant with Hague.

On March 24, Hennepin County Family Court found Hitomi Arimitsu in constructive contempt of all previous orders. As part of her purge conditions, Hitomi Arimitsu must return to U.S. or release our children to me on April 23 at the U.S. Consulate in Osaka. Tomorrow, April 7, Hitomi Arimitsu must surrender all passports of our children to the U.S. Consulate in Osaka, Japan, or communicate to the Minnesota court her intention to comply with the April 23 order.

On Monday and Tuesday, April 10th and 11th, the G7 Ministerial Foreign Affairs meeting will take place in Lucca, Italy. I hereby respectfully request that our Secretary of State, Rex Tillerson, brings the topic up during this important G7 meeting in order to have it subsequently discussed in the upcoming G7 summit that will be held in Italy on May 26th to the 27th.

Considering the two Italian children abducted and abused in Nagasaki shortly after moving to Japan in order to avoid Hague Convention proceedings, it is also in Italy's best interest to have this issue resolved before it is too late. The same goes for the other cases that each one of the G7 countries has pending with Japan. Yes, every G7 country has abduction cases that are going unresolved, and Japan stands in the way of these children being reunified with their parents. Kidnapping should not be a protected societal value.

Five days prior to the April 23 ordered return date, Vice President Pence will visit Japan on April 18th and 19th. He will meet his counterpart, Japanese Deputy Prime Minister Taro Aso. Vice President Pence will surely meet Prime Minister Shinzo Abe and Minister of Foreign Affairs Fumio Kishida as well.

I hereby respectfully request that Vice President Mike Pence speak with these Japanese officials and ask them to have Japan meet their international obligation to comply with the Hague Convention and return our children to their habitual residence in Minnesota. Excuses may be offered why they cannot, but I know from 30 years of involvement with Japan, Japan will force the return if required or given no other choice.

The following day, April 20, Italian Prime Minister Paolo Gentiloni will meet with President Donald Trump right here in Washington, DC. The significance of this is also related to the upcoming G7 summit. The host country has determining influence in setting the agenda of the G7 summit, and considering that citizen safety is the number one topic among the official priorities set by Italy for the G7 summit with a target area of managing human mobility, we would like to officially request to have child abductions in Japan, a form of human trafficking, discussed and included in the agenda.

I hereby respectfully request that President Donald Trump and Prime Minister Paolo Gentiloni talk about Japan's noncompliance with Hague Convention and resolve to put the issue on the G7 agenda. Japan's continuing failure to comply with international standards puts children in all G7 member states at risk of being abducted with no feasible means of recovery.

Japan remains an ongoing international threat to our children and our human rights. They are by all means victims of an outdated legal system. It is an opportunity for President Trump to demonstrate "America First" by demanding Japan respects a properly rendered decision and several return orders from a U.S. court.

There is no viable legal means at present to recover children through the Hague Convention if the taking parent in Japan refuses to cooperate with court orders, as I know well, and there are no consequences in Japan for contempt.

Our children remain with Hitomi Arimitsu in contempt of court with courts in both countries, aided and abetted by Mr. Yukinori Arimitsu of Arimitsu Industry Co., Ltd., of Osaka, Japan. I wonder if anyone in Japan has influence over Mr. Arimitsu to persuade him to end this conflict between Japan and the USA. Why would he want to put the country of Japan in jeopardy any longer?

Hitomi Arimitsu owes me approximately $95,000 in unpaid legal expenses and fines that have accrued since the time they were imposed by the Japanese legal system. The money remains uncollected owing to Japan's dysfunctional legal system. I wonder how any foreign party or government can feel their legal rights will be protected in Japan. There exists ample evidence of a dysfunctional judiciary, generating capricious rulings based upon pragmatism of situations, not principles of existing law.

There are good people and groups in Japan pushing for children's rights and Hague compliance. For example, Japanese Diet Representative Kenta Matsunami on March 8 of this year repeatedly asked the Japanese Minister of Justice, Katsutoshi Kaneda, whether he agreed with the interpretation of the revised Japanese Civil Code, Article 766, given by his predecessor, Satsuki Eda. At the time of those deliberations in the Judicial Affairs Committee, Mr. Eda stated that Article 766's meaning was to disqualify an abducting parent from custody preference. After a longwinded evasion of the question and repeated questioning by Mr. Matsunami, Mr. Kaneda was finally brought to respond in the affirmative, in English, "yes."

Likewise, Director General of the Japan Supreme Court Family Division, the Honorable Hitoshi Murata, acknowledged the statement of his predecessor at the time in 2011 when the revision of the Article 766 was being deliberated that the best interests of the child should be considered, and this has not changed since.

The revised Article 766 was designed to prevent abducting parents from retaining custody of their abducted children or gaining an advantage in court. Article 766 took effect 5 years ago and has been ignored by an unaccountable, rogue judiciary mired in tradition ever since.

On the same day the Hague Convention went into effect in Japan, April 1, 2014, the current Chief Justice of the Japanese Supreme Court, Itsuro Terada, assumed office as well. He issued a statement, and the translation reads, I quote:

> It becomes common for the courts to deal with cases which have to be considered domestic matters and international matters as the Hague Convention having come into effect today. So, I believe that we judges are asked to make sustained effort to meet the expectation and trust of the people in us and to tackle these matters by studying the real state of affairs happening in Japan and the international trend in order to strengthen the function of the judicial branch.

Shouldn't Japanese courts be following both the principle of the revised code Article 766, their domestic law, and the principle of the Hague Convention, their international obligation? In actuality, both legal standards are in abeyance in Japan. Japan's courts are not even functional for Japanese.

A case in point involves Mr. Yasuyuki Watanabe. Mr. Watanabe has battled in court many years to see his child. In an unprecedented decision, Matsudo, Chiba Family Court awarded Mr. Watanabe, a father, custody of their child, taking it away from the mother. This decision was appealed to the High Court on January 26 of this year, and the High Court overturned the previous decision in Matsudo.

The High Court ruling explicitly cited the old discarded legal standard, the continuity principle, a principle that rewarded the abducting parent with custody in order to not upset the child. The court ignored the 5-year-old Article 766, the current law. Mr. Watanabe is appealing this errant ruling to the Supreme Court in Japan.

Please note, joint custody is not a legal option in Japan, only sole custody. It is a zero-sum game in which the child is guaranteed to lose every time.

This abduction appears to have been well organized and well planned. We can see there is such activity by groups in Japan as described in a Liberal Time article about Shelter Net. There is also organized activity by radical left activists and communists in Japan. I believe these groups and their followers in Japan's judiciary were responsible for the noncompliant ruling of February 17. With more international pressure on Japan, groups such as these will be exposed and brought out of the shadows.

Now, I am required to go to the U.S. Consulate in Osaka for a second time to wait for our children to be released to me on April 23. Will the request by Vice President Mike Pence make a difference? Will Prime Minister Shinzo Abe, Foreign Minister Fumio Kishida, and Minister of Justice Katsutoshi Kaneda respond in kind and facilitate the return of our children?

I urge the Bureau of Consular Affairs in its annual Hague Compliance report, due by law on April 30, to reflect the failure to enforce Hague return orders once again in the Japan Country report. Moreover, I urge the report to finally categorize Japan as a noncompliant country.

Then, as indicated in the Goldman Act, Secretary of State Rex Tillerson ought to use his discretion to implement the most pernicious executive actions available to him by law, and specifically, extradition of our children and Hitomi Arimitsu to USA to appear in Minnesota court as repeatedly ordered. Secretary Tillerson possesses the character and stature to resolve this issue.

At a forum of the international community in which Japan takes part, this issue must be addressed at the G7 summit in Italy. Other G7 members must demand immediate changes to Japan's dysfunctional legal system and laws in order for Japan to be considered worthy of continued membership. It used to be G8, and it may be time for it to become G6.

In closing, I am here alone, but my voice represents not only my children and I, but hundreds of thousands of children, Japanese and foreign, that every year lose access to one parent in Japan. Japan has been complicit in ongoing retention of our children and failure to enforce several court orders.

Parental abduction is a penal crime in most advanced countries, but in Japan it is not. Japan cannot be trusted moving forward to voluntarily take steps necessary to effect functional enforcement of court orders of any kind, specifically Hague.

The tools exist in the U.S. Code to motivate Japan to comply. It is not a matter of ambiguity. The bright line has been blurred to suit others' interests, not the U.S., in the past. The Goldman Act provides a process and consequences in these situations. Within the Goldman Act there are a myriad of consequences to choose. The power to choose and impose these sanctions resides in one office, one official, one individual, Secretary of State Rex Tillerson.

Thank you again for this opportunity to speak before this committee. And I have tried to keep my testimony brief because I understand subcommittee members have family and perhaps even children they expect will be there when they return home.

[The prepared statement of Mr. Cook follows:]

James Cook   April 6, 2017   Washington, DC

Foreign Affairs Subcommittee on Africa, Global Health, Human Rights, and International Organizations

Thank you Chairman Smith, members of the subcommittee and members of the audience watching these proceedings all over the world. I really appreciate this opportunity to speak to you a second time about my Hague Convention case in Japan and the problems encountered following the previous testimony given last July.

First, I want to say hello to my children because I have not been allowed any access to them since August 2015. This is in direct violation of Hague and evidence of Japan's continuing noncompliance.

"Hello children. I have not and will not give up on having us together again in USA. I am sorry this situation has not been resolved by now. I am closer than ever before to having us together again. Please hold on. Love, Dad"

There were two failed Hague return enforcement attempts in Nara, Japan in Sept 2016. Direct enforcement was done exactly as Japan requires – an almost SWAT-like ambush where they are living.

During the direct enforcement, I was only able to hear the voices of our older sons and I did not recognize those voices. It was a sobering reminder of how much has been missed. As a parent, to be unable to recognize your own child's voice brings a type of pain that cannot be described, but certainly can be felt as a visceral shudder by all parents.

At the direct enforcement attempts, there were court officers, police, psychologists and officials from JCA and U.S. Consulate. With the exception of the U.S. officials, it was obvious that everyone else was there to protect the children from me trying to see them and to thoroughly document an anticipated, calculated failure. I foolishly thought these officials I had paid to execute direct enforcement were there for my success. In reality, they were just playing their roles towards a pre-determined outcome - failure.

Furthermore, it severely traumatized our children in a way that did not need to happen.

With the unsuccessful enforcement attempts, Japan has once again failed to enforce a Hague return order. This time it was the one issued from the Osaka High Court on January 28, 2016. This indicates a systemic problem that was also reported in the annual Hague Compliance report issued just a few days prior to my previous testimony in July 2016. Now it's two years in a row that Japan has been unable to enforce its' Hague return orders. This is a systemic problem and should be concerning for any foreign entity planning to enter into contracts or binding agreements with parties in Japan. It certainly should concern foreign governments regarding allowing any of their children to visit Japan.

Assumption of subject matter jurisdiction, in accordance with Osaka High Court's (OHC) return order dated January 28, 2016, and a mirror return order were issued from Hennepin

County Family Court, MN on December 2, 2016, again on December 13 2016, again on January 24 2017, and on March 24 2017 and then a very thorough analysis of continued subject matter jurisdiction and return order, April 4, 2017. Will Japan even respect our court's rulings, as we are all expected to respect theirs?

I was granted temporary sole custody and our children and they were ordered released to me on December 17, 2016 at the US Consulate in Osaka for their return to the United States. Our children were not brought to Consulate on that day, in violation of two Mn court orders. Hitomi Arimitsu was in contempt of the MN court orders that mirrored the Hague return order of Japan.

I must acknowledge the significant efforts and resources put into place by DoS to provide for a successful reunification at the Consulate on December 17th. I thank everyone involved!

After a year of unsuccessful enforcement, on January 5, 2017, Hitomi Arimitsu filed for a modification to OHC return order citing 'grave risk' standard under Hague. The evidence of grave risk cited was of relative lifestyle change if returned. On February 17, 2017, the Osaka High Court Hague return order of January 28, 2016 was revoked and at this time, our children are not being ordered returned by OHC.

The revocation of previous return order indicates an invalid interpretation of the Hague Convention and provides further evidence of Japan's failure to comply with its international obligation. Article 28 of the Japanese Hague implementing legislation enables an expanded interpretation of grave risk that gives judges' broad leeway, way beyond international precedent and language of Hague, to deny returns. In this instance, it overturned their own previous ruling and in effect made use of the taking parent's ongoing noncompliance with the Hague return order in Japan and from the habitual residence of the children in Minnesota.

Article 28 is not compliant with Hague and it must be ordered changed by fellow Hague signatories.

The February 17, 2017 decision was signed by:

Presiding Judge   Toru Matsuda
Judge   Yoshinori Tanaka
Judge   Takahiro Hiwada

We have appealed this ruling to the Japan Supreme Court and we received permission on March 29th to have our case heard. According to my attorney, it will likely take up to 1 month for the Supreme Court of Japan to receive our case file from OHC. If the February 17th decision is overturned, as we fully expect, it may take an additional 6-12 months for a Supreme Court hearing. The projected timeline far exceeds the expeditious processing of Hague cases as outlined in the Convention. My case began in August 2015 and it is still unresolved. Japan, in yet another way, is not compliant with Hague.

On March 24, Hennepin County Family Court found Hitomi Arimitsu in constructive contempt of all previous orders. As part of her purge conditions, Hitomi Arimitsu must return to USA or release our children to me by April 23rd at the US Consulate in Osaka. Tomorrow, April 7th, Hitomi Arimitsu must surrender all passports for our children to U.S. Consulate in Osaka,

Japan or communicate to Mn court her intention to comply with April 23 return order.

On Monday and Tuesday, April 10-11, the G7 Ministerial Meeting Foreign Affairs will take place in Lucca, Italy.

*** I hereby respectfully request that our Sec. of State Rex Tillerson brings the topic up during this important G7 meeting, in order to have it subsequently discussed in the upcoming G7 Summit that will be held in Italy on May 26-27. Considering the two Italian children abducted and abused in Nagasaki shortly after moving to Japan in order to avoid Hague Convention proceedings, it's also in Italy's best interest to have the issue resolved before it's too late. The same goes for the other cases that each one of the G7 countries has pending with Japan. Yes, every G7 country has abduction cases that are going unresolved, and Japan stands in the way of these children being reunified with their parents. Kidnapping should not be a protected societal value!

Five days prior to April 23rd ordered return date, VP Pence visits Japan April 18 and 19. He will meet his counterpart, Japanese Deputy Prime Minister, Taro Aso. VP Pence will surely meet Prime Minister Shinzo Abe and Minister of Foreign Affairs Fumio Kishida as well.

*** I hereby respectfully request that Vice President Mike Pence speak with these Japanese officials and ask them to have Japan meet their international obligation to comply with the Hague Convention, and return our children to their habitual residence in Minnesota. Excuses may be offered why they cannot, but I know from 30 years of involvement with Japan, Japan will force their return if required or given no opportunity to avoid.

The following day, April 20, Italian Prime Minister Paolo Gentiloni will meet with President Donald Trump in Washington D.C. The significance of this is also related to the upcoming G7 Summit. The host country has determining influence in setting the agenda of the G7 Summit, and considering that "Citizen safety" is the number 1 topic among the official priorities set by Italy for the G7 Summit with a target area of managing human mobility, we would like to officially request to have the child abductions in Japan discussion included in the agenda.

*** I hereby respectfully request that President Donald Trump and Prime Minister Paolo Gentiloni talk about Japan's noncompliance with Hague Convention and resolve to put the issue on the G7 agenda. Japan's continuing failure to comply with international standards puts children in all G7 member states at risk of being abducted with no feasible means of recovery. Japan remains an ongoing international threat to our children and their human rights. They are by all means victims of the outdated legal system. It is an opportunity for President Trump to demonstrate 'America First' by demanding Japan respects a properly rendered decision and return order from a U.S. court.

There is no viable legal means at present to recover children through the Hague Convention if the taking parent in Japan refuses to cooperate with court orders, as I know well, and there are no consequences in Japan for contempt. Our children remain with Hitomi Arimitsu, in contempt of courts in both countries, aided and abetted by Mr. Yukinori Arimitsu of Arimitsu Industry Co Ltd of Osaka, Japan. I wonder if anyone in Japan has influence over Mr. Arimitsu to persuade him to end this conflict between Japan and U.S.? Why would he want to put the country of Japan in jeopardy any longer?

Hitomi Arimitsu owes me approximately $95,000 in unpaid legal expenses and fines that have accrued since the time they were imposed by the Japanese legal system. The money remains uncollected owing to Japan's dysfunctional legal system. I wonder how any foreign party or government can feel their legal rights will be protected in Japan? There exists ample evidence of a dysfunctional judiciary generating capricious rulings based upon pragmatism of situations, not principle of existing law.

There are good people and groups in Japan pushing for children's rights and Hague compliance. For example, Japanese Diet Representative Kenta Matsunami, on March 8th, repeatedly asked Japanese Minister of Justice Katsutoshi Kaneda whether he agreed with the interpretation of the revised Japanese civil code article 766 given by his predecessor Satsuki Eda. At the time of those deliberations in the Judicial Affairs committee, Mr. Eda stated that Article 766's meaning was to disqualify an abducting parent from custody preference. After a long-winded evasion of the question, and repeated questioning by Mr. Matsunami, Mr. Kaneda was finally brought to respond in the affirmative, in English, saying "yes." Likewise, Director General of Japan Supreme Court Family Division, the Honorable Hitoshi Murata acknowledged the statement of his predecessor at the time in 2011 when the revision of article 766 was being deliberated that the best interests of the child should be considered, and this has not changed since.

The revised article 766 was designed to prevent abducting parents from retaining custody of their abducted children or gaining an advantage in court. Article 766 took effect five years ago, and has been ignored by an unaccountable rogue judiciary mired in tradition, since.

On the same day the Hague Convention went into effect in Japan, April 1, 2014, the current Chief Justice of the Japanese Supreme Court, Itsuro Terada, assumed office as well. He issued a statement that in translation reads

> "It becomes common for the courts to deal with cases which have to be considered domestic matters and international matters as the Hague Convention having come into effect today. So, I believe that we judges are asked to make sustained effort to meet the expectation and trust of the people in us and to tackle these matters by studying the real state of affairs happening in Japan and the international trend in order to strengthen the function of judicial branch."

Shouldn't Japanese courts be following both the principle of the revised civil code article 766, their domestic law, and the principle of Hague Convention, their international obligation? In actuality, both legal standards are in abeyance in Japan. Japan's courts are not even functional for Japanese.

A case in point involves Mr. Yasuyuki Watanabe. Mr. Watanabe has battled in court many years to see his child. In an unprecedented decision, Matsudo, Chiba Family Court awarded Mr. Watanabe, a father, custody of their child, taking it away from the mother. This decision was appealed to the High Court and on January 26th of this year the high court overturned the previous decision in Matsudo. The high court ruling explicitly cited the old, discarded legal standard-- the continuity principle. A principle that rewarded the abducting parent with custody in order to not upset the child. The court ignored the 5-year-old article 766, the current law. Mr. Watanabe is appealing this errant ruling to Supreme Court in Japan. Please note: joint custody is not a legal option in Japan, only sole custody. It's a zero sum game in which the child is guaranteed to lose every time.

This abduction appears to have been well organized and well planned. We can see there is such activity by groups in Japan as described in the Liberal Time article about Shelter Net. I believe these groups and their followers in Japan's judiciary were responsible for the noncompliant ruling of February 17th. With more international pressure on Japan, groups such as these will be exposed and brought out from the shadows.

Now, I am required to go to the US Consulate in Osaka for a second time to wait for our children to be released to me on April 23rd. Will the requests by Vice President Mike Pence make a difference? Will Prime Minister Shinzo Abe, Foreign Minister Fumio Kishida, and Minister of Justice Katsutoshi Kaneda respond in kind and facilitate the return of our children?

I urge the Bureau of Consular Affairs in its annual Hague Compliance report due by law on April 30th to reflect the failure to enforce Hague return orders once again in the Japan Country report. Moreover, I urge the report to finally categorize Japan as a non-compliant country. Then, as indicated in the Goldman Act, Secretary of State Rex Tillerson ought to use his discretion to implement the most pernicious executive actions available to him by law, and specifically, extradition of our children and Hitomi Arimitsu to USA to appear in Minnesota court, as repeatedly ordered. Sec. Tillerson possesses the character and stature to resolve this issue.

At a forum of the international community in which Japan takes part, this issue must be addressed at the G7 Summit in Italy. Other G7 members must demand immediate changes to Japan's dysfunctional legal system and laws in order for Japan to be considered worthy of continued membership. It used to be G8 and it may be time for it to become G6.

In closing, I am here alone, but my voice represents not only my children and I, but hundreds of thousands of children, Japanese and foreign, that every year lose access to one parent in Japan.

Japan has been complicit in the ongoing retention of our children and failure to enforce several court orders. Parental abduction is a penal crime in most advanced countries in the world, but it is not in Japan. Japan cannot be trusted moving forward to voluntarily take the steps necessary to effect functional enforcement of court orders of any kind, specifically Hague.

The tools exist in U.S. Code to motivate Japan to comply. It's not a matter of ambiguity. The bright line has been blurred to suit other's interest, not the U.S., in the past. The Goldman Act provides a process and consequences in these situations. Within the Goldman Act there are myriad of consequences to choose. The power to choose and impose these sanctions resides in one office, one official, one individual. Sec. of State Rex Tillerson.

Thank you again for this opportunity to speak before this committee and I have tried to keep my testimony brief because I understand committee members have family, and perhaps even children, they expect will be there when they return home.

Mr. SMITH. Mr. Cook, thank you so very much for again laying out your own case, but also with some very, very doable recommendations. And with the G7 meeting coming up, I think that is a tremendous opportunity for us to really rally with letters to Vice President Pence, the President, and to Rex Tillerson. And so I think your points were extremely well taken.

Dr. Frisancho.

STATEMENT OF AUGUSTO FRISANCHO, M.D. (FATHER OF CHILDREN ABDUCTED TO SLOVAKIA)

Dr. FRISANCHO. I would like to thank you, Chairman Smith and Ranking Member Bass and all the members of the subcommittee. I would like to say how this nightmare started. In 2008 my wife asked me for a divorce. I totally refused, and I told her we couldn't do this to the children. She told me, "You would give your life for your children but not for me. This is how you men think. When there is no longer love in the marriage, all you men want is to stay together only because of the children."

I asked her to try to work things out, seek professional help, get counseling, but nothing worked. After a year I accepted it. I did apologize to her for trying to keep our marriage alive. We agreed on joint custody, and I accepted her petition to go and together tell our children that we both have decided to divorce. However, we are still married.

Slovakia. In 2010, my wife abducted our children to Slovakia. I filed an application for the return of the children under the Hague Convention on the Civil Aspects of International Child Abduction. My wife was called upon by the Central Authority for the Hague Convention in Slovakia to discuss the peaceful return of our children home. When no agreement could be reached, the case was sent to the Slovak court for Hague legal proceedings that continue to this day.

My wife acknowledged in court that the children love their father, and at the end the Slovak courts ruled the return of the children to the United States, but they never enforced it. A court order that was once final and binding was reopened later, and the case continues to this day.

Travel ban. The Slovak courts also prohibited the removal of our children outside of Slovakia until the Hague proceedings were finished, but my wife, in violation of that travel ban, removed our children to Hungary.

European Court of Human Rights. Later on, I filed a complaint against Slovakia under the European Court of Human Rights in Strasbourg where a chamber of seven judges unanimously ruled that Slovakia had violated my human rights as a father with respect for my family life, and it ordered Slovakia to pay me damages. This court concluded that there was no dispute that the relationship between the father and his children was one of family life. The Slovak ruling can by no means be said to have been in the children's best interest.

So where are we now? Three judges in the United States, four in Slovakia, and seven judges in Strasbourg, a total of 14 judges, men and women from different backgrounds and countries, all have acknowledged that the abduction of our children is wrong. However, the Slovak courts have stayed the Hague proceedings on the mistaken presumption that Slovakia no longer has jurisdiction, and currently the Slovak Constitutional Court is reviewing my appeal.

Slovakia needs to comply not only with the Hague Convention, but also with the European treaty called Brussels II that gave Slo-vakia the tools to order again the return of the children to the U.S. and enforce that order in Slovakia in the event that the children are found in Slovakia or to cooperate with any other country mem- ber of Brussels II, such as Hungary, to have the Slovak court order enforced in that third country. How can we start a new litigation in Hungary when Slovakia has already accumulated evidence dur-ing 6 years?

Criminal charges. To top all that injustice, my wife is trying to file in Slovakia criminal charges against me for unpaid child sup-port for children who, according to the Slovak courts, say no longer reside in Slovakia. I have said in the past that by doing that I would be supporting this emotional abuse of the children, and, moreover, it is the U.S. court that has jurisdiction over the chil-dren. This court has given full custody, legal and physical, to me, and it says that child support will be decided by the Baltimore court, not by Slovakia.

Access to my children. I have repeatedly obtained court rulings ordering the mother to allow the children to meet with me. I trav-eled multiple times to Europe. In 1 year alone, I took 14 weeks off from my work trying to stay in touch with my children. With the court orders in my hands, I went to my wife's parents' house, and my children's grandmother, Mrs. Piroska Kiss, told me, "Don't you know, Augusto, that you will never see the children again? Go away. Stop bothering us."

On another occasion, I filed a missing persons report in Slovakia, but not even the law enforcement will help me see the children. I went to their schools repeatedly in both Slovakia and Hungary, met with the teachers and principals, who introduced me to my children's classmates in their classrooms, but I couldn't see the children. I never saw my children because my wife had taken them away for days and weeks until she learned that I had returned to the United States.

The courts also ordered my wife to let me Skype, email, and talk over the phone with our children, but she declared openly in the court that she didn't have a computer, she didn't have Internet, and she will never let me see "her" children anyway.

My boys need me. Every boy needs his father. They are teen-agers. Their bodies and minds are changing from boys to men.

Besides being father and sons, we were friends. We had a very strong, respectful, and very much a loving relationship. When my wife had stayed at work from early morning to late evenings, our children stayed with me all day long.

I did everything with them. Woke them up. Got them ready for school. Gave them breakfast. Made lunch boxes. Drove them to school. Then I ran to work and left my job early in order to pick the boys up from school. Then we had lunch and rested, played, did the sports. Then we went home back, and while the older boys were doing homework, I did art, drawing with Raymi, my little son. Then we had dinner together, showered before going to bed, prayed, and got ready for sleeping. And when the lights went off, I would tell them stories until they fell asleep.

Once it happened that while I was talking to them about life and that one day we would go to heaven, one of my boys asked me, "But, Daddy, why do we have to go if this life is so beautiful?"

I am sorry. I am just sharing with you this because I would like you to know that my children had a good life in the United States. They attended one of the top schools in the Nation.

And before all this idea of divorcing came up and the kidnapping, I had concerns about my wife's mental health. She collapsed in the parking lot of our children's schools and was taken to a psychiatric hospital where she was retained against her will and put on strong antipsychotics.

After she was released, she described to me that she said there that she was sick because of her boss, so that all the guilt will go on her boss' shoulders, because she fought with her boss and she resigned her job. A mother of three children one day came to my house saying, "I resigned." I said, "What happened?" "Well, I had a fight with my boss, and I told her I don't need the job."

We were actually in that time making the same amount of money. We had to pay credit cards, a mortgage, two cars, private schools, and my salary would not suffice for all that, and she knew that. But she just resigned from her job. That is indicating how she was mentally.

She raised accusations against some of our children's teachers, neighbors, pediatricians, dentists, and other people. One year prior to the abduction, she went to Slovakia supposedly to rest, but later on she emailed me saying if I could come quickly to Slovakia to pick her up because she could no longer live under the same roof with her parents. According to her, everybody in the village where they lived looked at her as she was a criminal because of the complaints her father, Mr. Alexander Kiss, had made against her.

Department of State, Office of Children's Issues. I would like to express my gratitude to the Department of State for having assisted me from day one. U.S. Embassy officials attended each and every hearing in Slovakia. They sent diplomatic notes and demarches to the Slovak Government and had personal meetings with government officials.

However, as we all can see, although this tremendous work done by the Department of State is very much appreciated, after almost 7 years my sons have still not returned home. This is showing us that much more needs to be done.

The Department of State could use the additional tools provided by the Goldman Act in order not to let Slovakia find excuses to release its responsibility by saying that it no longer has jurisdiction over my children's Hague return case, forgiving my wife for removing our children to Hungary in violation of a travel ban, and staying the proceedings in Slovakia.

We are not telling Slovakia how to rule their judicial system, but we are demanding Slovakia to follow the rules of treaties for which Slovakia had signed a membership, with all due respect to Slovakia.

Specifically, the Department of State could take the following actions, as we all know. Delay or cancel bilateral working, official, or state visits and student exchanges with Slovakia. Withdraw, limit, or suspend United States development, economic, or security assistance.

In summary, the Goldman Act not only empowers the Department of State, but it even requires punitive actions against countries that do not respect international agreements like Slovakia.

Acknowledgements. I would like to express my gratitude to the Department of Justice, FBI, and INTERPOL, especially to Senator Cardin and Congressman Elijah Cummings for their support; to Mr. Ausias Orti Moreno, who is here, my children's case manager from International Social Services; and to the National Center for Missing and Exploited Children who has been helping me from day one, especially to Rami Zahr, Sarah Baker, Team Hope Program Director Abby Potash, all present here. To all my friends, members of church, colleagues from work, from Hopkins, my lawyers. They have left their jobs today to be here with me.

My very special thanks to you, Chairman Smith, and your counsel Allison Hollabaugh.

I would like you to know that when I spoke to my children over the phone just shortly after the abduction, they naively asked me, "Daddy, can you help us return home?" My heart breaks every time I remember these words. I promised my children then that I was going to do whatever was only possible in the world to help them. During these past 7 years I have been working with lots of people, but one thing I can say about you, Chairman Smith, is that I can sense that you have sincere compassion for our children. You, indeed, care for the well-being of the children who are victims of all kinds of abuse committed by their own parents as a result of their blind selfishness. Abductors put themselves first, children are secondary, and often use this as an act of revenge against the spouse.

But this is why the law exists. What would the world be today if there were no laws? So on behalf of my three boys, thank you, Mr. Smith, for creating the Goldman Act. Thank you for asking the Department of State to enforce the Goldman Act and request Slovakia and all the other countries who today are still attempting to bypass the law to go ahead and simply fulfill the law and return our American children.

We did the same for them. When a child was kidnapped to the United States by a parent, our authorities made sure the child was safely returned to the left-behind parent in Slovakia. We did not create excuses. We acted fast, and we used all the possible resources and will do it again.

I know that I have very short time, but just one paragraph to my children.

To you, Ork'o, Amaru, and Raymi, this is the first time I have been given the opportunity to talk to you since our phone conversations were cut in 2010. I love you guys with all my heart. You are my life. I miss you.

Every morning when I get up, I kneel and pray to God to help us to be together again, to protect you from any evil. I kiss your picture that I have placed on the door of the fridge. I keep your picture on my cell phone. I dream about you often, but I see you in my dreams as still little as you left our home almost 7 years ago. I bet you are bigger and stronger today.

Hang in there, guys. Stay strong. Dad loves you more than anything in the world. I live only for you. Forgive me for not having been able to honor my promise to help you return home until today.

And please now read my blog, read the court orders. I will put them all online. Read the news. Please give me the chance to tell you my part of the story, too. Every story has two sides. You have heard only one side. No matter what you have been told about me, please listen also to me.

You guys also pray to God all the time and pray for your mother, too. God doesn't do anything wrong, but he only permits bad things to happen. I am waiting for you and will always be.

Te amo Ork'o. Amaru te adoro. Raymi, I love you. Papa.

[The prepared statement of Dr. Frisancho follows:]

Testimony of J. Augusto Frisancho, M.D.
Father of three children abducted to Slovakia in 2010

Before the U.S. House of Representatives,
Committee on Foreign Affairs
Subcommittee on Africa, Global Health, Global Human Rights and
International Organizations

Hearing: ***Enforcement in Not Optional***: *The Goldman Act to
Return Abducted American Children*

April 6, 2017

My three sons Raymi, Amaru & Ork'o abducted to Slovakia in 2010

My name is Augusto Frisancho, I would like to thank you Chairman Smith, Ranking Member Bass, and all the Members of the Committee on Foreign Affairs for giving me this unique opportunity to be here on behalf of my children.

How the nightmare started
In 2008 my wife asked me for a divorce. I totally refused and told her we couldn't do this to the children. She told me: "You would give your life for your children, but not for me, this is how you men think. When there is no longer love in the marriage, all you men want is to stay together only because of the children." I asked her to try to work things out, seek professional help, go to counseling, but nothing worked. After a year, I accepted it. I did apologize to her for trying to keep our marriage alive, we agreed on joint custody and I accepted her petition to go and together tell our children that we both had decided to divorce.

On August 25, 2010, my wife asked me to take care of our children for three days as there was something she needed to do. She asked me to wait for them at a park. I left my work at Johns Hopkins and waited at that park until it got dark. She never arrived. I dialed all existing numbers but they were all disconnected. I drove to many places where I thought they could be. The next day I learned that she had abducted our children to her home country, Slovakia, with the assistance of her parents.

It takes two people to divorce, as it takes two to be in a marriage, everybody would acknowledge that. But **no parent has the right to emotionally abuse their children by removing the second parent from their children's lives**. Abducting parents have no rights to psychologically manipulate innocent children by making them believe the left-behind parent is a bad person. Of course, there are circumstances that must be considered like physical abuse, sexual abuse, addictions, etc. but none of these conditions existed in our relationship.

Slovakia
The day after the abduction, I filed an application for the return of the children under an international treaty, the Hague Convention on the Civil Aspects of International Child Abduction. My wife was called upon by the Central Authority for the Hague Convention in Slovakia to discuss the peaceful return home of the children. When no agreement could be reached, the case was sent to the Slovak court for the Hague legal proceedings that continue to this day.

Hague return order without enforcement:
The Slovak judges told the mother she did not have the right to remove our children from everything they were used to, their home, their school, their friends, that those were American children and that if she had matrimonial problems with her husband, she had to return to Baltimore and solve those issues on US ground because only US judges had jurisdiction over that and over the children. The judges also said that the

mother was unable to prove her allegations of abuse on the part of the father. My wife acknowledged in court that the children love their father.
The Slovak courts ruled the return of the children to the USA, but they never enforced it.

Hague case reopened:
The Hague return order that was final and binding was reopened later and the case recommenced, which caused the extension of the proceedings for years. I attended almost all of the hearings. My wife attended some at the beginning, but later on she missed the majority of them.

Judge wants to see the children:
The mother brought only two of the boys to court but not the third child. **Judge was concerned because of the children's appearance** and ordered to see them again in the presence of a psychologist and a translator because the children do not speak the Slovak language. However, the mother repeatedly failed to bring our three children to court. That was actually the **last time the mother showed up in court!**

Travel ban:
The Slovak courts prohibited the removal of the children outside of Slovakia until the Hague proceedings for their return to the US were finished. **In violation of that court-ordered travel ban, my wife wrote to the Slovak court that the Slovak court had forced her to leave the country, and she had had to move to Hungary.** In Hungary, she said that she did not know where the father was, she requested to receive monetary assistance for the poor. She changed her and our children's citizenship to Hungarian. However, I, the father, am the custodial parent. Foreign officials could just google my name to find me online due to the kind of work I do and would easily find my email address, phone number, etc.

Hague proceedings stayed:
The Slovak courts stayed the proceedings twice, even after I appealed. The Hague case is currently being reviewed by the Slovak Constitutional court, but there is no time limit for this court to give a response. In the past, **it sometimes took about one year for the Slovak court located in Komarno to issue a response.**

European Court of Human Rights (ECHR)
Although the Slovak courts acknowledged the wrongful removal of our children, ordered their return to the US under the Hague Convention, their ruling became final and binding within the meaning of Slovakian law, and its enforcement was ordered, the courts never carried out the enforcement order. It took them years to deal with the case, allowing my wife to file dozens of motions, complaints, appeals and extraordinary appeals on points of law and other legal procedures that only gave her time to continue this emotional abuse of our children and to orchestrate her next abduction to Hungary. I filed a complaint under the ECHR, where **a chamber of seven judges unanimously ruled that Slovakia had indeed violated article 8 of the Convention and my human**

34

rights as a father with respect for my family life, and it ordered Slovakia to pay me damages.

The ECHR concluded that:

-) There was no dispute that the **relationship between the father and his children was one of family life.**

-) **Slovakia** as a Contracting State of the Hague Convention **is obligated to carry out the** proceedings for the **return of the children** unless there are circumstances preventing the children's return, **allowing the courts in the country of their** alleged **habitual residence (USA) to resolve** all questions relating to **parental rights and responsibilities.**

Proceedings in Slovakia **should be practical and effective.**

-) The ECHR notes in particular the opinion expressed by the President of the Bratislava First District Court, who said that there is a systemic problem in that numerous appeals are allowed during the return proceedings, with the effect of negating the purpose of the Hague Convention. The recommended Hague proceedings bear witness to these systemic concerns.

Thus, <u>the status of the children has not been determined by any court</u>, the courts in Slovakia having no jurisdiction to do so, and the courts in the country of their alleged habitual residence (USA) having no practical opportunity to do so, **a state of affairs which <u>can by no means be said to have been in the children's best interests.</u>**

Where are we now?

The Slovak Constitutional Court is reviewing the case, it will decide whether it supports the staying of the Hague return proceedings ordered by the First Instance Court and upheld by the Regional Upper Court, or if it will reopen the case and remit it back for further proceedings as it did in 2012.

In any case, we have solid legal grounds to file another complaint against Slovakia under the ECHR. But what is the point of having all these court rulings on our side, what is the purpose of "winning" the case again at the ECHR, and receiving again money for damages from the government of Slovakia if our main goal of helping the children return home has not been accomplished?

Three judges in the US, four judges in Slovakia, and seven judges at the ECHR in Strasbourg, a total of 14 people, men and women from different backgrounds and countries, all have acknowledged that the abduction of our children in wrong, but the children are still being emotionally abused for almost 7 years!

Slovakia needs to rule consistently with the ECHR. Slovakia **needs to comply not only with the Hague treaty but also with the European treaty called Brussels II Regulation**, that gives Slovakia the tools **to order again the return of the children** to the US **and** to enforce that order in Slovakia in the event that the children are found in Slovakia, or **to cooperate with any other country member of Brussels II, such as Hungary, to have the Slovak court order enforced in that third country.**

How can we start new litigation in Hungary when both Slovakia and Hungary are members of the same treaty? A Slovak court order must be enforced in Hungary or vice versa. **The most important reason not to file again in Hungary is that Slovakia has already accumulated evidence during six years!**

After all our attempts to convince Slovak authorities to fulfil their obligations to resolve abduction and access cases, and after the final judgement of the ECHR from July 2015, Slovakia made amendments to its laws concerning international abductions to Slovakia effective as of January 2016. None of these new regulations, however, apply retroactively to rule against the return of my children to the US following Brussels II Regulation and cooperation with Hungary for the final enforcement.

To top all that injustice, **my wife is trying to file criminal charges against me for unpaid child support for children Slovak courts say no longer reside in Slovakia.** I have said in the past that by doing that, I would be supporting this emotional abuse of my children. Moreover, it is **the US court** that has jurisdiction over the children. This court **has given full custody, legal and physical, to me, and in its custody ruling, it says that child support will be decided by the Baltimore court, not by Slovakia.**

Access to children

I requested of the Slovak courts access to my children while the Hague proceedings for their return to the US were taking place. I had repeatedly obtained preliminary rulings ordering the mother not only to physically prepare the children to meet with their father, but also to psychologically promote visitation in order to prevent alienation. I **travelled several times to Europe, in one year alone I took 14 weeks off from my work at Johns Hopkins trying to stay in touch with my children.** With the court orders in my hands, I went to my wife's parents' house. Her parents threatened to call the police. My children's grandmother, **Mrs. Piroska Kiss, told me: "Don't you know, Augusto, that you will NEVER see the children again?** Go away and give us peace, stop bothering us." I then called the police and showed them the court order. They spoke with the grandparents, who told the police they did not know where the children nor their daughter were. On another occasion, I filed a missing person report in Slovakia, but not even law enforcement would help me see my children. I went to their schools repeatedly in both Slovakia and Hungary and met with the teachers and principals, who introduced me to my children's classmates in their classrooms and gave me a tour of the school. **I never saw my children because my wife had taken them away for days and weeks until she learned I had returned to the US. The courts also ordered my wife to let me skype, email and talk over the phone with our children, but she refused to obey the court rulings, saying that she does not have a computer nor internet.** She changed the house phone number and **declared openly in court that she will never let me see "her" children.**

For more than a year, the US Consul tried to visit and bring to my children gifts that I brought from the US and left at his office. My wife would always refuse to accept his visit, until one day after he persisted, she agreed to accept with his visit and **received a letter from me for our children and the gifts. The Consul asked her if the boys could talk to me using his cell phone and if he could take a picture of them for me, but my wife refused that.**

My boys need me. Every boy needs his father. They are teenagers, their bodies are changing from boys to men, their minds are changing. **Besides being father and sons we were friends, we had a strong, respectful, very much attached and loving relationship.** When my wife stayed at work from early morning to late evenings, our children stayed with me. I did everything with them, woke them up, got them ready for school, gave them breakfast, made lunch boxes, drove them to school, then I ran to work, and left my job earlier in order to pick the boys up from school. Then we had lunch, rested, played, and did sports like soccer or baseball depending on the season. My oldest son did karate since he was 6 years old. We then went home, and while the older boys did homework, I did art or drawing with Raymi, the little one. Then we had dinner together, showered before going to bed, prayed and read before sleeping. Once the lights went off, I would tell them stories until they fell asleep. Sometimes I would fall asleep first, but they woke me up and I continued telling the story.

Once it happened that while I was talking to them about life and that one day we will go to heaven, one of the boys asked me: **"But Daddy, why should we go if this life is so beautiful"....** I am sharing this with you so that you see what a good life our children had before the idea of divorcing came up.

Concerns about my wife's mental health

We are still married. My wife filed for divorce here in the US, her mother served the summons on me, and when I read all her accusations and the kind of financial compensations she was asking, I just could not believe her mind was right. Once she kidnapped our children to Slovakia, she dismissed her motion for divorce in Baltimore and filed another one in Slovakia, but I responded **I did not want a divorce, but to remain married so that when the children return to the US, she could also return with them** and that I will support her until she starts working again.

She collapsed in the parking lot of our children's school, and because she screamed aloud using profanity in front of the children and their parents, the principal called 911 and an ambulance. She was taken to a psychiatric hospital where she was retained against her will and put on strong antipsychotics. After she was released, she described to me how it was when she was in the hospital and would comment that she said there that she was sick because of her boss, so that all the guilt will go on her boss's shoulders. However, later she changed the version and blamed me, her husband, for everything. She raised accusations against some of our children's teachers, she wanted to change our children's pediatrician, and dentist.

In order to cover the real reasons for abducting our children, in Slovakia she said that I had forced her to leave the US. In Slovakia, she fought with the judge and requested the judge to be removed from the case. One of her lawyers wrote a letter to the court explaining that she abandoned representation of the case. After all, when she abducted our children to Hungary, she wrote to the Slovak court that Slovakian authorities, judges, lawyers, and law enforcement officials all forced her to leave the country and find refuge in another country. One year prior the abduction, she went to Slovakia, supposedly to rest after she fought with her boss in Baltimore and resigned her job. Later on, she emailed me asking me to quickly travel to Slovakia to pick her up because she could no longer live under the same roof with her parents. According to her, everybody in the village where they lived looked at her as if she was a criminal due to the complaints her father Mr. Alexander Kiss had made against her, and people in the village felt sorry for her parents and thought she was a bad daughter.

I am disclosing all this because I would like you to understand **why I am concerned about my wife's mental instability.** I mentioned that in the local court in Komarno, however, judge Konkolovska responded that although the father had taken the liberty to put in doubt the mother's mental health, she was healthy; otherwise, she would not be able to perform her job.

What judge Konkolovska does not take into consideration is that **one can be mentally ill and still be able to work** if his or her problem-solving abilities are not affected, **one can know how to solve work issues that are encountered on a daily basis, but this does not mean the person is mentally fit.**

Department of State – Office of Children's Issues (DOS - OCI)

I would like to express my gratitude to the DOS – OCI for having assisted me from day one, as follows,

-) For helping me file an application for the return of my children to the US.

-) **Embassy officials attended each and every hearing in Slovakia.**

-) OCI requested that Slovakia provide an explanation for the delay in proceedings.

-) **Embassy officials sent diplomatic notes to the Slovak Ministry of Foreign Affairs (MFA)** at senior levels. The MFA informed the US Embassy Bratislava that the MFA **would continue to monitor the case.**

-) **U.S. Ambassador to Slovakia** joined ambassadors and chargés from other European embassies in Slovakia to participate in a multilateral effort with senior officials from Slovakia's Ministry of Justice to **encourage Slovakia's compliance with the Hague Convention.**

-) Embassy officials met with working-level Slovakian counterparts.

-) OCI reported a Pattern of Noncompliance, and the **Embassy delivered a demarche to the Government of Slovakia noting Slovakia's** citation in the 2015 Annual Report on International Parental Child Abduction as demonstrating patterns of **noncompliance,** meaning that thirty percent or more of the total international abduction cases in Slovakia remained unresolved at the end of the reporting period.

-) **Embassy officials met with the representatives of the Slovak Ministry of Justice** Legislative Department **responsible for** civil and commercial law and the **recent changes to the Family Code and Civil Procedural Law to improve Slovakia's compliance with the Convention.**

-) Slovakia made amendments to its laws concerning international abductions to Slovakia effective as of January 2016. None of these new regulations however, apply retroactively to rule again the return of my children to the USA, following Brussels II Regulation and cooperation with Hungary for the final enforcement.

I'd like to tell officials from the DOS OCI that I am grateful for what CI has done up to now. However, I would very much appreciate if OCI could use the additional tools provided by the Goldman Act in order not to let Slovakia find excuses to release its responsibility by saying it no longer has jurisdiction over my children's case, forgiving my wife for removing our children to Hungary in violation of a valid travel ban court order and staying the Hague proceedings in Slovakia. Instead, have Slovakia follow Brussels II regulations, continue the Hague case in Slovakia, order again the return of American children home, and enforce its ruling with the cooperation of their counterparts in Hungary. **We are not telling Slovakia how to rule their judicial system, but we are demanding Slovakia to follow the rules of treaties for which Slovakia had signed a membership.**

OCI could still take the following actions:
-) Have the US Special Advisor for Children's Issues meet with Slovak authorities.
-) Make an official public statement condemning the unresolved case of US children.
-) Delay or cancel bilateral working, official, or state visits and student exchanges.
-) Withdraw, limit, or suspend United States development, economic, or security assistance.
-) In the 2015 Annual Report on International Parental Child Abduction (IPCA), table 4 on page 30 shows Countries Demonstrating Patterns of Noncompliance: Slovakia is listed there and in the Description of pattern of noncompliance **it is not mentioned that Law enforcement authorities failed to locate the children and enforce orders of rights of access rendered by the judicial authorities** in abduction cases (D). Also, that the Slovak courts failed to implement and comply with the provisions of the Convention (C). The pertinent information in the report should be corrected.

The Goldman Act not only empowers the Department of State but it even requires punitive actions against countries that do not respect their international agreements like Slovakia.

Acknowledgements

I'd like to express my gratitude to the Department of Justice, FBI and Interpol, to Ausias Ortí Moreno, my children's case manager from International Social Services, to National Center for Missing and Exploited Children, especially to Rami Zahr, Sarah Baker, and Team Hope Program Director Abby Potash, all present here. And on behalf of my children, my very special thanks to you, Congressman Smith, and your Counsel, Allison Hollabaugh. When I spoke to my children over the phone shortly after the abduction, they naively asked me: **And Daddy, "can't you help us return home?"** It was as if they were saying: you are our father, how come you can't help us? My heart breaks every time I remember those words. I promised my children then, I was going to do whatever was only possible in the world to help them. My children are the reason why I live; they were and will always be the most precious thing God has entrusted to me. Since 2010 I have been working with lots of people, and one thing about you that I can say, **Chairman Smith, is that you have sincere compassion for all children, you indeed care for the well-being of all the children who are victims of all kinds of abuse committed by their own parents as a result of their blind selfishness.** Abductors put themselves first, children are secondary and often used as an act of revenge against the spouse. But this is why the law exists. What would the world be today if there were no laws? So, on behalf of my three boys, thank you Mr. Smith for creating the Goldman Act, thank you for asking the Department of State (DOS) to enforce the Goldman Act and request Slovakia, and all the other countries who to date are still attempting to bypass the law, to go ahead and simply fulfil the law and return our American children home. We did the same for them, when a child had been kidnapped by a parent to the US, our authorities made sure the child was safely returned to the left behind parent in Slovakia. We did not create excuses. We acted fast, we used all the possible resources and will do it again.

To my children

And to you, Ork'o, Amaru and Raymi, this is the first time I have been given the opportunity to talk to you since our phone conversations were cut in 2010. I love you guys with all my heart, you are my life, I miss you. Every morning when I get up, I kneel and pray to God to help us be together again, to protect you from any evil. I kiss your pictures that I have placed on the door of the fridge, I kiss your picture on my cell phone, I dream about you often, but I see you in my dreams still little, as you left our home almost 7 years ago. I bet you are bigger and stronger now. Hang in there guys, stay strong, Dad loves you more than anything in the world, I live only for you. Forgive me for not having been able to honor my promise to help you return home until today. And please, read my blog, read the news, read the court orders, please give me the chance to tell you my part of the story too, every story has two sides, you have heard only one side. No matter what you have been told about me, listen also to me, please. You guys also pray to God, all the time, pray for your mom too. God does not do anything wrong, but He permits bad things to happen. I am waiting for you and will always be.
Te amo Ork'o. Amaru te adoro. Raymi, I love you.
Papa.

Raymi

41

Raymi plays T-ball

Raymi's graduation - preschool

Raymi

44

Amaru

Amaru plays baseball

Amaru

47

Ork'o

Ork'o

Ork'o

I love you guys! With all my heart!

Dad

April 6, 2017

Mr. SMITH. Dr. Frisancho, thank you very much for your testimony. It is very moving, and hopefully it will soon result in the return of your children, and we will do everything we can.

Dr. FRISANCHO. Thank you very much.

Mr. SMITH. I would like to now ask to present his testimony Mr. Jagtiani.

And thank you for being here.

STATEMENT OF MR. VIKRAM JAGTIANI, CO-FOUNDER, BRING OUR KIDS HOME (FATHER OF CHILD ABDUCTED TO INDIA)

Mr. JAGTIANI. Thank you, Honorable Chairman Smith, members of the subcommittee, and Congress. Thank you for giving me the opportunity to testify before this subcommittee today.

I wish none of us had to testify on an issue like parental child abduction, but given the serious humanitarian crisis affecting thousands of children and families in America and around the world, I feel privileged to be able to speak about my daughter's abduction from her home in New York to Mumbai, India, and the challenges many other left-behind parents and myself have faced in securing her return home.

Chairman Smith, with your permission, I would like to submit my full testimony for the record.

Mr. SMITH. Without objection.

Mr. JAGTIANI. Thank you.

My testimony today centers around our children. They are a product of love, and during their development, it is critical for our children to receive the unconditional love of both parents. Even if the parents decide to part ways, it is wrong to rob a child the love of and access of the other parent. Any problems that occur between a mother and father as they part ways have to be worked out in an orderly fashion through a court in the home jurisdiction. Abducting the child and using them as a pawn for revenge or as leverage is incorrect and unacceptable.

In my case, my daughter, Nikhita, was abducted to India, a non-convention, nonbilateral country, in September 2013, when she was only 4 years old. Nikhita didn't know she was being abducted, nor could she have prevented her own abduction.

This is the stark reality of International Parental Child Abduction (IPCA), which many governments around the world, including India, fail to acknowledge. Today, India has new leadership, and it is my hope that the new leadership will see this as an urgent problem and tackle it in the right way, so that these cases get resolved. Just as the U.S. had a civil rights leader in Dr. Martin Luther King, India had Mahatma Gandhi. Both these leaders had human rights and social justice at the forefront of their campaigns. If Gandhi were alive today, he would support India's accession to The Hague Convention on Civil Aspects of International Child Abduction.

At the time of the abduction, my wife and I had been living separately, but we shared custody of Nikhita, who had just been enrolled at a new school on Manhattan's Upper East Side for the academic year 2013-2014. My daughter was abruptly removed from school by the mother, citing a family emergency. Nikhita's mother took a leave of absence from her job, terminated her lease, and traveled to Mumbai, India, on a one-way ticket, coincidentally on the very day my dear father passed on in India.

I happened to be visiting my ailing father in Mumbai at the time, and after his final rites and mourning period, I returned to my home and my job in New York. My estranged wife, meanwhile, announced that she would not be returning, nor would she permit the child to travel back with me. She had unilaterally decided to relocate to Mumbai because, she claimed, her career prospects looked brighter there, and she alleged Mumbai was her birth and matrimonial home now.

Nothing could be further from the truth. She is a U.S. citizen, who abducted a U.S.-born and raised child, both of whom—both of whose habitual residence was in New York. My estranged wife was attempting to move the playing field to a favorable forum, and using our child as a pawn to gain from her wrongful act. It was a sinister plan, and I avowed to fight for my child's rights.

On returning to New York, I heard from her friends that she had been planning this abduction for months, so I immediately consulted a lawyer and initiated a wrongful removal and custodial interference complaint. Due to the challenges by the abducting parent, it took me 18 months to complete service in India, upon which she became party to the custody case in New York.

The court conducted a detailed investigation. I was awarded temporary custody, and my estranged wife was directed to immediately return Nikhita to New York. Of course, she has not complied. As a result, Nikhita's mother has been charged with kidnapping by the Federal prosecutors in the Southern District of New York.

A battle is won or lost by choosing the terrain on which it will be fought. While thwarting service of New York proceedings and orders, Nikhita's mother embarked on a series of malicious civil and criminal proceedings in India, not only against me, but against members of my extended family. With an array of favorable laws and an extensive support base in India, Nikhita's mother has relentlessly pursued a slandering campaign in multiple courts and multiple jurisdictions.

Jurisdictional arbitrage is the practice of taking advantage of discrepancies between competing legal jurisdictions using whatever tactics and loopholes imaginable.

For those on the receiving end, India can feel like the wild, wild west, and abducting parents in India play a nefarious game by filing false, unsubstantiated criminal charges in India, while in my case, using the local police to harass my extended family.

Interestingly, India is a signatory to The Hague Convention on Service of Process of Judicial Documents, a founding member of The Hague Conference, but is not a signatory to The Hague Convention on Civil Aspects of International Parental Child Abduction. This has resulted in unnecessary hardships, wrongful separations of children from their loving parents, legal delays, and prohibitive costs.

Challenges in India: Based on recent press reports, more than 27 million cases are pending in India's district courts, 6 million of which have lasted longer than 5 years, while another 4½ million are waiting to be heard in the high courts. The former esteemed Supreme Court Justice of India, B.N. Agrawal, stated, "Delay and disposal of cases not only creates disillusionment among the litigants, but also undermines the capability of the system to impart justice in an efficient and effective manner."

Abducting parents and their aiders use India's systemic delays in the judiciary as a tool to benefit from their wrongdoing, seeking to delay or deny the return of abducted children to the countries of their habitual residence.

Left-behind parents face other major hurdles. India's institutional bias against recognizing parental child abduction as a violation of human rights and law, and gender stereotypes, which manifest itself in various forms. Indian judiciary and policymakers view international parental child abduction not as a child's rights issue and legal violation, but rather, as routine child custody issues. When a mother perpetrates child abductions, they often treat these cases as women's rights issues, the result being Indian courts routinely relitigate the divorce and child custody cases decided by competent courts in other nations where children habitually resided, thus creating a complex legal web.

When mothers of Indian origin, regardless of their nationality, abduct children to India, they are often viewed as helpless women, or Abla Naaris, who cannot legally defend themselves in a foreign country and, hence, need protection in mother India.

When a father abducts children to India, left-behind mothers often face other forms of gender bias. Left-behind mothers are asked by Indian courts to return to India to fulfill their duty to their children and spouses.

Often, Indian courts usurp jurisdiction and issue arbitrary orders without framing of issues or examining evidence that then become cumbersome to remove. Ex parte interim orders are often issued without due process, lingering for years, compounding the pain for the seeking parent and the child.

When a mother abducts children and flees to India, there are a whole cocktail of legal procedures to avail of, and numerous nefarious operators to advise them. Two of the most commonly misused and Draconian laws are related to the Protection of Women Violence Act 2005, and Section 298 of the Indian Penal Code. While the intent of many of these laws may be good, quite often during implementation, the spirit is lost, when lines get blurred between allegation, fact, imagination, and reality. It is no wonder that parents, regardless of gender, who abduct their children to India, find safe haven under Indian laws. In all cases, children are the innocent victims of a crime that India refuses to recognize.

My family and I are victims not only of IPCA, but of India's legal system, which is failing to deliver justice. My daughter is an innocent voiceless victim of a crime committed by her mother, aided and abetted by India's refusal to recognize IPCA's child abuse, a human rights violation, and a crime. I am left with no choice but to litigate in a broken legal system and a cross-border legal vacuum, trying to reunite with my only child, my daughter, Nikhita.

For the last 3 years, since the passage of the Goldman Act, we at Bring Our Kids Home have been tirelessly advocating for the Indian and U.S. Governments to work together to address the pain and suffering caused by the lack of legal framework that deals with the serious and growing issue.

For our part, the many left-behind parents have successfully obtained U.S. court orders establishing our children with habitual residence of the United States and were wrongfully removed from the United States, or retained in India. Starting in December 2012, the Department of State has sent formal written requests to India's Ministry of External Affairs, and our Government has engaged with the powers in India to provide a commonsense solution to have our children returned. However, the State Department, the Department of Justice, and others, have failed to convince our strategic partner, India, to cooperate with us in the return of American children. The institutional and systematic complacency in India, and the lack of urgency by both our Governments to decisively address this serious and growing issue, only hurts our children and our national interests.

We are a rule-of-law-based society, but when it comes to international parental child abduction to India, there is no rule of law. During Prime Minister Modi's visit to the U.S. in June 2016, we were pleased to note that the issue of international parental child abduction was raised in the strategic dialogue and was part of the bilateral statement.

> Recognizing its mutual goal of strengthening greater people-to-people ties, the leaders' intent to renew efforts to intensify dialogue, to address issues affecting the citizens of both countries that arise due to differences in the approaches of legal systems, including issues relating to cross-country marriage, divorce, and child custody.

Shortly after, we saw reports that the Ministry of Women and Child Development, MWCD, posted a draft bill for India's accession to The Hague Convention on Child Abduction on their Web site and we were hopeful and excited to witness progress. Bring Our Kids Home provided feedback and comments to help guide a fair and commonsense solution for our kids.

Early in the fall of 2016, we heard sound bites that the vested interests in India, including the National Commission for Women, prominent women's rights attorneys, and abducting parents were lobbying to maintain the status quo and convince the Ministry of Women and Child Development to oppose its own draft IPCA bill. Sure enough, by Thanksgiving, we received news reports that they had junked their draft IPCA bill and would not sign The Hague Convention, the reason stated being, we found that there are more cases of Indian women who returned to the safety of their homes in India after escaping a bad marriage. Cases of women who are foreign citizens married to Indian men going away with their children are far fewer. Hence, signing The Hague Convention would be a disadvantage to Indian women. Also, a majority of such cases pertain to women instead of men running away, said a Women and Child Development official.

As you can imagine, we had a pretty dismal holiday season without our children and being robbed of our hope of any solution at all.

Five weeks later, on January 3, 2017, we saw a report that India will reconsider the hasty decision and invite all stakeholders to a meeting on February 3, 2017. As important stakeholders, we reached out to the Ministry of Women and Child Development through multiple channels, only to be informed that this would be a closed inter-ministerial rule meeting, and the MWCD suggested we participate via Twitter. After pushback from several left-behind parents on Twitter, the ministry tweeted an email address in a couple of days before the start of the consultation, but would not disclose the precise time and venue of the consultation, which would be a significant impact to the lives of our children and families.

Bring Our Kids Home and several left-behind parents emailed our concerns and suggestions to the Ministry to consider during the IPCA Hague consultation held on February 3, 2017. Based upon independent sources who attended the consultation in New Delhi, we were informed that mothers who had abducted American children to India were at the consultation, and even presented at the event. However, no representation from left-behind parents was invited. I was aghast to find out that amongst those who presented at the Ministry of Women and Child Development consultation was my estranged wife, who made a detailed presentation on why India must not accede to The Hague Convention on Child Abduction, and presented a perverse narrative on IPCA.

Thus, over the past several months, left-behind parents have been on an emotional and psychological roller coaster, while the Government of India gives mixed signals at best and the U.S. Government offers no substantive relief. Left-behind parents across the spectrum feel like we are fighting a David-versus-Goliath battle, and our administration isn't pulling its weight in this fight.

Before I conclude my testimony, I would like to make a direct appeal to Prime Minister Modi, to Foreign Minister Swarage, to Minister Menaka Gandhi, and to policymakers and judges in India. Instead of dehumanizing us left-behind parents, who have had our children taken away from us, been robbed of the love and affection of our children in the best years of their lives, most often being denied any access, and, in my case, the abducting parent will not even disclose the physical location of my child in Mumbai, it is heartbreaking when I receive a message from my Indian attorney the morning of a scheduled Skype call with my daughter that she is too busy with her friends or her activities to come to the phone or the computer to say hello.

This could happen to anyone. Imagine it was your child. Please engage with us, not symbolically, but as important stakeholders, and allow us to participate in creating a fair and just policy so that no parent or child has to go through this trauma we have endured.

In conclusion, I respectfully ask you, Chairman Smith and Members of Congress, is enforcement of the U.S. law optional? How long should we, parents of America's stolen children, wait for our Government to enforce our laws and hold perpetrators accountable?

How many more hearings do we need before countries like India, Japan, and Brazil be held accountable for their lack of cooperation in returning American children?

We have a new President who puts America first. I urge President Trump and our Federal agencies to enforce the Goldman Act and put America's children first above other bilateral priorities. With Prime Minister Modi's possible trip to the U.S. in May of this year, I respectfully urge President Trump to use this opportunity with Prime Minister Modi to resolve this issue as a bilateral priority and usher a new era of bilateral friendship between our two countries.

Please help bring my Nikhita back. Please help bring all our children home. Thank you.

[The prepared statement of Mr. Jagtiani follows:]

Vikram Jagtiani
Parent of Child Abducted to India in 2013
Testimony before the House Committee on Foreign Affairs, Subcommittee on Africa, Global Health, Global Human Rights, and International Organizations
The Goldman Act to Return Abducted American Children: Enforcement is not Optional
April 6, 2017

Honorable Chairman Smith, Ranking Member Bass and Members of the Committee and Congress. Thank you for giving me the opportunity to testify before this Committee today. I wish none of us had to testify on an issue like parental child abduction, but given the serious, humanitarian crisis, affecting thousands of children and families in America and around the World, I feel privileged to be able to speak about my daughter's abduction from her home in New York to Mumbai, India and the challenges I and many other left behind parents have faced in securing her return home.

My testimony today centers around our children – they are a product of love, and during their development it is critical for our children to receive the unconditional love of both parents. Even if the parents decide to part ways, it is wrong to rob a child the love and access of the other parent. Any problems that occur between a mother and father as they part ways have to be worked out in an orderly fashion through a court in the home jurisdiction. Abducting the child and using them as a pawn for revenge or as a leverage is incorrect and unacceptable.

In my case, my daughter Nikhita, was abducted to India, a non-Convention, non-bilateral treaty Country, in September 2013, when she was only 4 years old. Nikhita didn't know she was being abducted, nor could she have prevented her own abduction. This is the stark reality of International Parental Child Abduction (IPCA), which many Governments around the World, including India, fail to acknowledge.

Today India has a new leadership and it is my hope that the new leadership will see this as an urgent problem and tackle it in the right way, so that these cases get resolved. Just as the US had a great civil rights leader in Dr. Martin Luther King, India had Mahatma Gandhi. Both these leaders had human rights and social justice at the forefront of their campaigns. If Gandhi were alive today, he would support India's accession to the Hague Convention on Civil Aspects of International Parental Child Abduction.

At the time of the abduction, my wife & I had been living separately but we shared custody of Nikhita, who had just been enrolled at a new school on Manhattan's Upper East Side for the academic year 2013-14. My daughter was abruptly removed from school by her mother, citing a family emergency. Nikhita's mother, took a leave of absence from her job, terminated her lease, and travelled to Mumbai, India on a one-way ticket – coincidentally on the very day my dear father passed on in India. I happened to be visiting my ailing father in Mumbai at the time and after the final rites and mourning period, I returned to my home and my job in NY. My estranged wife meanwhile announced that she would not be returning nor would she permit the child to travel back with me. She had unilaterally decided to relocate to Mumbai because she claimed, "her career prospects looked brighter", and that she alleged, "Mumbai was her birth and matrimonial home". Nothing could be further from the truth. She is a U.S. citizen, who abducted a U.S. born and raised child, both of whose habitual residence was in NY. My estranged wife was attempting to move the playing field to a favorable forum and using our child as a pawn to gain from her wrongful act. It was a sinister plan and I vowed to fight for my child's rights.

On returning to NY, I heard from her friends that she had been planning this abduction for months, so I immediately consulted a lawyer and initiated a wrongful removal and custodial interference complaint. Due to challenges by the Abducting parent, it took me 18 months to complete service, upon which she became party to the custody case in NY. The court conducted a detailed investigation, I was awarded temporary custody, and my estranged wife was directed to immediately return Nikhita to New York. Of course she has not complied. As a result Nikhita's mother has been charged with kidnapping by Federal prosecutors in the Southern District of New York.

A battle is won or lost by choosing the terrain on which it will be fought. While thwarting service of NY proceedings and orders, Nikhita's mother, embarked on a series of malicious civil and criminal proceedings in India, not only against me, but against members of my extended family in India. With an array of favorable laws and extensive support base in India, Nikhita's mother has relentlessly pursued a slandering campaign in multiple courts and multiple jurisdictions. Jurisdictional arbitrage is the practice of taking advantage of discrepancies between competing legal jurisdictions – using whatever tactics and loopholes imaginable. For those on the receiving end, India can feel like the "wild, wild West" and abducting parents in India play a nefarious game by filing false, unsubstantiated criminal charges in India, while as in my case, use the local police to harass my extended family.

Interestingly, India is a signatory to the Hague Convention on Service of Process of Judicial documents, a founding Member of the Hague Conference, but is not a signatory to the Hague Convention 'on Civil Aspects of International Parental Child Abduction. This has resulted in unnecessary hardships, wrongful separations of children from their loving parents, legal delays and prohibitive costs.

Challenges in India – Urgent need for reform

Based on recent press reports, more than 27 million cases are pending in India's district courts – 6 million of which having lasted longer than 5 years while another 4.5 million are waiting to be heard in the High Courts. A former esteemed Supreme Court of India Justice B N Agrawal stated: *"Delay in disposal of cases, not only creates disillusionment amongst the litigants, but also undermines the capability of the system to impart justice in an efficient and effective manner."* Abducting parents and their aiders/abettors use India's systemic delays in the Judiciary as a tool to benefit from their wrongdoing, seeking to delay or deny the return of abducted children to their countries of habitual residence.

Left behind parents, face another major hurdle, India's institutional bias against recognizing parental child abduction as violation of human rights and law, and gender stereotypes, which manifests itself in various forms:

- Indian Judiciary and Policymakers view international parental child abduction, not as a children's rights issue and legal violation, but rather as "routine child custody" issue. And when mother's perpetrate child abductions, they often treat these cases as women's rights issue. The result being, Indian Court routinely relitigate divorce and child custody cases, decided by competent courts in other Nations where children habitually resided, thus creating a complex legal web.

- When mothers of Indian origin, regardless of their Nationality, abduct children to India, they are often viewed as "helpless" women (or "Abla Naaris") who cannot legally defend themselves in a foreign country, and hence need protection in "Mother India".
- When father's abduct children to India, left behind mothers often face other forms of gender bias. Left behind mothers are asked by Indian Courts to "return" to India to fulfill their "duty towards their children and spouse".
- Often, Indian Courts usurp jurisdiction and issue arbitrary orders without framing of issues or examining evidence that then become cumbersome to remove.
- Ex-parte interim orders are often issued without due process, linger for years, compounding the pain for seeking parent and the child.
- When a mother abducts children and flees to India, there is a whole cocktail of legal procedures to avail of, and numerous nefarious operators to advise them. Two of the most commonly misused and draconian laws are related to the Protection of Women Violence Act 2005 & Section 498A of the Indian Penal Code. While the intent of many of these laws may be good, quite often during implementation the spirit is lost, when the lines get blurred between allegation, fact, imagination & reality.

It is no wonder that parents, regardless of gender, who abduct their children to India, find safe haven under Indian laws. In all cases, children are the innocent victims of a crime, that India refuses to recognize.

Recently in a PIL (Public Interest Litigation) to amend some draconian laws, the petition stated – "It is a common feature of many laws, enacted ostensibly for women's protection and strengthening of women's rights, that in practice they tend to negate the presumption of innocence, a founding principle of Indian criminal jurisprudence and arm the police with enormous powers of arrest and harassment, thus jeopardizing life and liberty."

My family and I are victims not only of IPCA, but of India's legal system, which is failing to deliver justice. My daughter is an innocent, voiceless victim of a crime committed by her mother, aided and abetted by India's refusal to recognize IPCA as child abuse, a human rights violation and a crime! I am left with no choice but to litigate in a broken legal system and a cross border legal vacuum, trying to reunite with my only child, my daughter Nikhita.

For the last 3 years since the passage of The Goldman Act, we at Bring Our Kids Home, have been tirelessly advocating for the Indian and U.S. Governments to work together to address the pain and suffering caused by the lack of a legal framework that deals with this serious and growing issue. For our part, the many left behind parents have successfully obtained US Court orders establishing our children were habitual residents of the United States and were wrongfully removed from the U.S. or retained in India. Starting in December 2015, the Department of State has sent formal written requests to India's Ministry of External Affairs, and our Government has engaged with powers in India to provide a commonsense solution to have our children returned. However, the State Department, the Department of Justice and others have failed to convince our "Strategic Partner", India to cooperate with us in the return of American children. The institutional and systemic complacency in India, and the lack of urgency by both our governments to decisively address this serious and growing issue only hurts our children our National interests. We are a rule of law based society, but when it comes to international child abductions to India, there is no rule of law!

During PM Modi's visit to the U.S. in June 2016, we were pleased to note that the issue of IPCA was raised in the strategic dialogue, and was part of the bilateral statement [Joint Statement Link]:

"48) Recognizing its mutual goal of strengthening greater people-to-people ties, the leaders intend to renew efforts to intensify dialogue to address issues affecting the citizens of both countries that arise due to differences in the approaches of legal systems, including issues relating to cross-country marriage, divorce and child custody."

Shortly after we saw reports that the Ministry of Women & Child Development ("MWCD") posted a draft bill for India's accession to The Hague Convention on Child Abduction, on their website [refer to link Draft Bill and Notice]. We were hopeful and excited to witness progress.

Bring Our Kids Home provided feedback and comments to help guide a fair and common-sense solution for our kids. Early in the Fall of 2016 we heard soundbites that the vested interests in India, including the National Commission for Women (Indian Government funded entity), prominent women's rights attorneys and abducting parents, were lobbying to maintain the status-quo, and had convinced the MWCD to oppose its own Draft IPCA Bill. Sure enough, by Thanksgiving we read news reports [refer to link] that they had "junked" their draft IPCA Bill and would not sign The Hague Convention. The stated reason being:

"We found that there are more cases of Indian women who return to the safety of their homes in India after escaping a bad marriage. Cases of women who are foreign citizens, married to Indian men, going away with their children are far fewer. Hence signing the Hague Convention would be to the disadvantage of Indian women. Also, a majority of such cases pertain to women instead of men running away", said a WCD official"

As you can imagine we had pretty dismal holiday season without our children and being robbed of our hope for any solution at all.

Five weeks later, on January 3, 2017, we saw a report that India will reconsider their hasty decision and invite all the stakeholders to a meeting on Feb 3, 2017. As important stakeholders, we reached out to the MWCD through multiple channels, only to be informed that it would be a "closed inter-ministerial meeting", and, the MWCD suggested we participate via Twitter. After push back from several left behind parents on Twitter, the Ministry tweeted an email address a couple of days before start of the "consultation", but would not disclose the precise time and venue of the "Consultation" which would a significant impact to the lives of our children and families.

Bring Our Kids Home and several left behind parents emailed our concerns and suggestions to the Ministry to consider during the IPCA/Hague "Consultation" held on February 3rd, 2017. Based on independent sources who attended the "Consultation" in New Delhi, we were informed that, mothers who had abducted American children to India were at the "Consultation" and even presented at the event. However, no representation from left behind parents was invited. I was aghast to find out that amongst those who presented at the MWCD "Consultation" was my estranged wife, who made a detailed presentation on why India must not accede to The Hague Convention on Child Abduction and presented a perverse narrative on IPCA.

Thus, over the past several months, left behind parents have been on an emotional and psychological roller coaster; while the Government of India gives mixed signals at best; and the U.S. Government offers no substantive relief. Left behind parents across the spectrum feel like we are fighting a "David vs. Goliath" battle and our Administration isn't pulling its weight in this fight.

Before I conclude my testimony, I'd like to make a direct appeal to PM Modi, to Foreign Minister Swaraj, to Minister Menaka Gandhi, and to policy makers and judges in India. Instead of dehumanizing us left behind parents, who have had our children taken away from us, been robbed off the love and affection of our children in the best years of their lives, most often been denied any access, and in my case the abducting parent will not even disclose the physical location of the child in Mumbai. It's heartbreaking when I receive a message from my Indian attorney, the morning of a scheduled Skype call with my daughter – that she is too busy with her friends or her activities, to come to the phone or computer to say "Hello". This could happen to anyone, imagine if it was your child! Please engage with us, not symbolically, but as important stakeholders, and allow us to participate in creating a fair and just policy, so that no child or parent has to go through this trauma we have endured.

In conclusion, I respectfully, ask you, Chairman Smith and Members of Congress, "Is enforcement of U.S. Law optional"? How long should we, parents of America's stolen children, wait for our Government to enforce our laws and hold perpetrators accountable? How many more hearings do we need, before countries like India, Japan, Brazil and others are held accountable for their lack of cooperation in returning American children?

We have a new President, who puts America First. I urge President Trump and our Federal Agencies, to enforce the Goldman Act, and to put America's Children First, above other bi-lateral priorities. With Prime Minster Modi's, possible trip to the U.S. in May of this year, I respectfully urge President Trump to use this opportunity with Prime Minister Modi, to resolve this issue as a bilateral priority and usher a new era of bilateral friendship between our two nations.

Please help bring my Nikhita back - Please help bring ALL our children home!

Thank you!

Mr. SMITH. Mr. Jagtiani, thank you very much for your testimony and for your appeal to Prime Minister Modi. When he was here last year, I actually introduced him to one left-behind parent, a young woman whose two children, two sons were abducted, and asked him personally to intervene. I have met with the Ambassador. There has been a pushback on all of these cases, which is deeply troubling.

And my first question is that the Goldman Act provided a very, I believe, effective framework, but it requires faithful implementation. We got less than adequate implementation under the Obama administration. It is unclear whether or not President Trump will faithfully implement it. I hope and pray that he does. When he met with Prime Minister Abe, we sent a detailed letter to him before that meeting regarding the left-behind parents, the older cases, as well as the new Hague cases, both of which are being inadequately cared for by the Japanese Government. And I would just point out that in 2011, when I went to Japan with Nancy and Miguel Elias on behalf of their grandchildren, Jane and Michael, we met with the Minister of Foreign Affairs, he was then the Vice Minister, Matsumoto, and he was very empathetic. We found empathetic ears, but not empathetic actions on the part of individuals. The Eliases now are still waiting many years later, the abduction was right before Christmas 2008. And so many other of the longer cases have been agonizing beyond words.

Then last year, a couple years ago, at the first oversight hearing of what OCI was doing in terms of its report, it was an embarrassment, how poorly crafted the report was, how it left out critical details and information, so bad that they went back and said they would redo it, and it came back better, but certainly not covering the fullness that we had hoped that they would.

In 2016, for example, Japan was not listed as a country demonstrating a pattern of noncompliance, despite the fact that it hit all of the criteria that should have put them on that list, which would have then led to the hoped-for sanctions to sharpen the minds of our friends in Japan; and they noted that there was a problem with enforcement of return orders, exactly what Mr. Cook has raised to us today.

Enforcement of Goldman is first. That, we can do. And Goldman was not enforced by the Obama administration, and I find that to be a missed opportunity. And for all of you, it must be agony beyond words, because there were tools that were unutilized and remained in the toolbox.

Dr. Hunter, you had a successful case, thank God, and we have three individuals whose cases remain unresolved. I would ask all of you, first the report has to be done right. The April 30 deadline has been missed before. Last year, it was 72 days late. And, frankly, I would rather have lateness and tardiness than an inadequate report. So my hope is that they will get it right this year. And Japan certainly jumps off the page. India needs, I think, a much more robust response once it is so designated as a noncompliant country. So getting it right on the report, and, Dr. Hunter, you might want to lead off on that.

One of the things that I found appalling was a pattern with the last administration in not speaking truth to power.

I also authored, besides the Goldman Act, the Trafficking Victims Protection Act, and that requires a report every year that lays out countries along a tiered system, Tier 3 being egregious violators. Well, 16 countries were improperly given a passing grade by the Obama administration. And I am not saying here what I didn't say then. I had a series of hearings at which we said, how could you falsify the report on sex and labor trafficking to give Malaysia, Oman, China, and other countries, Cuba, a passing grade because of other political considerations? The report has to get it right and state clearly and without any ambiguity where the country stands, list the cases honestly. And I can tell you if the report comes out inadequate again, no matter what comes out in the report, we will have a hearing on that to hold whoever the new person is to account and to encourage that at least get the report right done first, and then the sanctions regime and enforcement and the imposition of penalties will be part two, which is the way the law designed it. I am very concerned as well that there were no MOUs. When I was in Japan with the Eliases, we raised with our delegation there, the Ambassador was out of the area then, but we raised it repeat- edly since, and with every other country where there are individual left-behind parents who, when a Hague, for example, was entered into, are left behind a second time, because obviously Hague is from the date of ascension, and anyone before that is not covered by Hague.

So we have pleaded with the Obama administration to enter into MOUs with countries to figure out a mechanism to get those children back home to their left-behind parents. Not a one. Not a one. We also wanted that for countries that are not part of the Hague Convention, because obviously, there needs to be a durable mechanism for effectuating the return of those children, and you need a system; the bottom line is to make that happen. And, so, I am very, very concerned about that. But I have brought it up and when Prime Minister Modi, if he does come again, that is something we will appeal to the administration to raise.

So the idea of the report, MOUs, and this issue—and, again, Mr. Cook, your idea of the G7 is a fantastic one. We will circulate letters. I know that Allison brought that up earlier today at the meeting at the White House. I do hope that the White House—you know, of all things, when the theme that the Italians have put for this, citizen safety, well, how about the safety of abducted children? That should jump off the page. Your thought of a G6, that was an interesting and very novel idea as well.

So speak to the reports, getting them right. Again, I would rather miss the deadline and get it right. They are 72 days late last year and didn't get it right on a number of countries, like Japan. Then I will yield to my friend and colleague, and we will have some additional questions after that.

Dr. Hunter.

Ms. HUNTER. Thank you, Mr. Chairman. And the reporting is essential for a few reasons. One, transparency is important for us as parents, who have been advocating for this.

So in my professional capacity, data drives our decisions. I work for the Kentucky Office of Highway Safety. We use data about driver behavior, vehicle miles traveled, fatalities, serious injuries. We rely on data to address the solutions and to drive our solutions. And so, it is very, very important that we aren't, in my professional capacity, doing what we think needs to be done; we are relying on good, quality information. And that is something that we have been, for some time, asking the State Department and the Office of Children's Issues for.

Part of that, we have begun to take it into our own hands, and we are trying to collect data from parents to help us to fully identify the scale and scope of this problem. We were very pleased at the White House meeting to learn this morning that there are indeed mechanisms and analytical tools that are available. So we are hopeful.

And from iStand's position, there is not much that can be done about what has happened. What we can do is look at a way forward. And for us, the ability for the State Department to clearly, accurately, honestly, and with integrity, report on the full scope and scale of the problem is essential. And I would venture to say that once there are true numbers out, that will mean great things for Congress, and your ability to effectively advocate for your constituents as a casework function, but then also, to effectively engage with nations, but we can't know any of that until there is proper reporting. And so we do call upon the State Department as they issue the next report to make sure that the information is reliable and it is consistent, and if it is reliable and consistent, these worst-offending countries are going to rise straight to the top. We are going to see Japan as noncompliant, we are going to see Brazil as noncompliant, we are going to see India as noncompliant. Even the countries that aren't signatories, if the information is reported accurately, the United States will be in a position of strength, the President will be in a position of strength when he engages with these nations to effectively advocate for American children.

And if I might just very briefly say on MOUs (Memoranda of Understanding) or other types of agreements, these are essential. It is our understanding that this administration has, for all intents and purposes, thrown out the playbook about how it has been done and multilateral agreements and multilateral treaties. We are in favor of that. We are in favor of the United States negotiating directly with every single nation individually and from a position of strength. We have many, many tools in our arsenal in the Goldman Act to require countries to return our children, and I think that there ought to be both that dialogue, and that has its place, but, yes, strongly worded memoranda that make it uncomfortable for countries.

Mr. COOK. One of the ideas I have scribbled down here and I left it out of my testimony, but it would be wise and would make a statement if the State Department were to come out and issue a travel warning, specifically for the country of Japan, and as the United States, indicating that we do not recommend anybody, any children of half Japanese descent, or anybody that has a child of that to travel out of the United States at any point, because to circumvent The Hague, the latest gimmick, if you will, is—what is happening is that, let's say a Japanese spouse will play all nice and say, can we just go visit my family in Japan? Okay. Let's just take a vacation, which to a compassionate and understanding U.S. citizen might say, sure, let's go visit the family.

Once you are in Japan, it is done. She can have you arrested, or he, excuse me, but it is mostly women, so put it that way. She can have you arrested. And as we know, too many cases of people that get held for 23 days in the Tokyo hotel, and other things like that. And so that, one, sends a statement, symbolic; two, it is very practical sense, because good-hearted, compassionate people are being hoodwinked into returning with their children to Japan, and at that point, they are just like this individual from Italy, he went back and everything turned suddenly. And there is nothing that can be done at that point, because we all know The Hague is ineffective once you are in Japan.

Mr. JAGTIANI. Yes, Chairman Smith. We thank you so much for your efforts, you know, in engaging with India's leaders on behalf of Bindu Philips and with Prime Minister Modi and the Indian Ambassador. We heard you used to get him in the halls at Rayburn, and we thank you so much for that. And actually, Bindu is in India right now, I think visiting her kids, after 8 years, she had an order from the Supreme Court of India to be able to see them. And they have now actually aged out of the system, which is really pretty tragic.

As I was actually talking to Dr. Hunter off the record, one of the issues with India is we effectively are dealing with cultural biases, and we have to change the thinking before we can solve the problem. And it is a long haul, but I think with the tools within the Goldman Act now, soft diplomacy might not work as well. So we need to do something to really get them to take some action on our orders here. And it is my hope that President Trump, who is a family man, will take cognizance of this issue in the upcoming visit, and we will see some resolutions. Thank you, sir.

Mr. SMITH. Mr. Garrett.

Mr. GARRETT. Thank you, Mr. Chairman.

It strikes me—and I will tell you by way of background, that I spent about 10 years as a criminal prosecutor, and when I finished law school, I swore never to do domestic law. I would rather try a murder case. And I mean that, and I don't mean it to be funny. A couple of times during the testimony today, Mr. Chair, I had very itchy eyes that needed wiping. The circumstances are just heartbreaking. I want to commend the folks who came, I believe probably with Dr. Frisancho. You obviously have a good strong support network, a lot of people here on your behalf.

It strikes me that perhaps wording, as it relates to the status of your respective children, might get in the way of messaging. And what is beyond my ability as a father and a divorcee of two children to wrap my brain around, is not that you don't have custody of your children—and I am going to tell you how I feel, not perhaps what you want to hear—it is that you are not able to see your children.

And as I think through this process in my limited tenure here, Mr. Chairman, and members of the panel, I try to think about what outcomes are possible, what can we get to. And so what I will promise you that our office will do is reach out, specifically starting with Japan, to the Ambassadors and Embassies and start to ask questions. And I say starting with Japan, because obviously Slovakia and Brazil and India are other nations of note, but my questions won't be driven toward gaining custody of your children, it will be driven toward gaining the right of you to see your children, right? Because there are two sides to every case, the court can come to whatever conclusion it wants, but to deny you the right to even see your children is beyond my ability to wrap my brain around. It is a grave injustice not only to yourselves, but to your children.

Dr. Hunter, you talked about the scope of the problem. And there is a handout up here that we haven't received, I am going to ask if our office can be made privy to, but I want to wrap my brain around that, if you all have amalgamated data on what countries have how many U.S. dual-citizen children residing. What is the scope of the problem? And I don't know if there is an answer to that except for I am asking for your data so that we can wrap our brains around it.

Do you know a number off the top of your head? Ms. HUNTER. We know numbers, but we are concerned about the accuracy of those numbers. And we truly believe that they have been low-balled, so to speak.

The State Department reports that every year, about 1,000 American children are abducted, and taken to a foreign nation, where it is a fight to bring them home. However, we suspect those numbers are much higher, for a few reasons. One, many, parents don't know that they need to report. They feel when their child has been abducted, that either if they can't solve it themselves, there is no hope. And so we know that there are probably cases in which children don't report.

We have been able to quantify the numbers. And we like to look at this from a whole-number perspective. So over the last 5 years or so, we can imagine that over 5,000 children have been taken. My colleague, Jeffery Morehouse, from Bring Abducted Children Home, they often indicate that over the span of the time that the Office of Children's Issues was established, 29,000 children have been abducted, and a fraction of those have come home.

But to your answer, Mr. Garrett, we don't know, which is why I am actually optimistic that now that—that we know that the State Department has this reporting ability, perhaps we can get more accurate numbers, and there are many data points that we could parse out of that.

Mr. GARRETT. Well, a number obviously is a number, but a name and a face are compelling, and so I would encourage you, and I will work with the chairman to try to—and obviously there are privacy concerns, we are dealing with minors, but at least as it relates to the specific Members of Congress, compile a list. I would love to know the names, dates of birth, and dual nationality status of the young people from my congressional district. I encourage you to send to each Senator and Congressperson the list, because names and faces make people move. Numbers are scary. But I am asking if you guys can do that, starting with us, and that will help us have a jumping-off point; not that someone by virtue of living in my district is any more important than any of you, but we have a limited amount of bandwidth.

Mr. Cook, you talked about the legal process in Japan. I am vaguely familiar with the barriers to entry to the legal profession in Japan. And suffice it to say, we have an awful lot of lawyers in this country who might not be practicing law if they were subject to the requirements of the Japanese bar. It can't be cheap. Do you have a dollar figure? I heard $96,000 at some point.

Mr. COOK. Well, with respect to the situation going on in Japan legally and culturally, there are several things that I can't disclose or say.

Mr. GARRETT. But how much have you spent? And if you can't disclose that, that is fine.

Mr. COOK. It is a lot.

Mr. GARRETT. So what I am driving at here is——

Mr. COOK. I quoted a $95,000 figure. That is some time in history. That is not a current.

Mr. GARRETT. Right. So what I am driving at here—and this is bound to be a cottage industry in the legal profession in Japan of people who represent foreigners who have children in Japan.

Mr. COOK. Yes.

Mr. GARRETT. And I don't begrudge them, although I think they owe you a duty of forthrightness on the front end, that it is a tough system and that the results aren't guaranteed. What I am driving at here, though, is that if you are not able to earn the amount of money required to fight the fight that you are fighting, you have got nothing, right? I mean, and that——

Mr. COOK. Well, Mr. Garrett, here is a case in point: I am virtually without financial means anymore. And after a year of trying to enforce the return order of the Osaka High Court of over a year ago, that drained significant assets that I had. In fact, lost our house in the process. Okay?

Well, the loss of the house and my drained financial resources was used as the primary rationale for the Osaka High Court to revoke their order of return, because, "He has no money, why would you send him back to America?" And that fundamental, and so, in essence, they just wait you out. They want you to quit legally, financially, emotionally, spiritually. And that has been allowed to occur, primarily because we have had a Department of State unwilling to use the Goldman Act tools that it has had.

A view, since you come from the legal background, a view to the enforcement in Japan, and I use the term "enforcement" loosely, every step of the way for me to have—first of all, to have access to my children, I require the abductor, my wife's, permission. In order to do the direct enforcement or do the ambush, we needed her permission to do it that day.

So I ask you, what do you think the likelihood is I am going to have access to my children if the legal foundation in Japan requires the permission of the abductor to allow me to do it? And there is nobody to enforce that, and so Japan will be in indefinite noncompliance with The Hague.

Mr. GARRETT. Have any of you on the panel had any contact, even via telephone or mail or email, with your children, or is it just radio silence, to use a military sort of cliche?

Mr. JAGTIANI. Yes, I have, actually. There was a court order for me to get Skype access. Initially it was phone, and then they escalated it to Skype, which I got, but that has been discontinued now over the last couple months.

Mr. GARRETT. Well, again, I pride myself on not telling people what I think they want to hear, but the truth, and I will tell you that you have enlisted a warrior for your cause today in the form of myself and our office, but my goal is not to fight for you to receive sole custody, my goal is to fight for you to receive access, because the courts will arbitrate who the custodial parent is, what have you, but I can't fathom that you have no access.

Mr. JAGTIANI. Yep.

Mr. GARRETT. And I think that requires the light of day be shown on these circumstances, and that the fourth estate be enlisted, and that we shame them, if you will, into simply allowing you access.

Mr. COOK. Currently in Japan, there is an evolving, I will call it a scandal, I am going to the heading called Shelter Net, but I can't get into the details too much, because it is not my country, but it is being slowly handled. And I alluded to it in my testimony about there are forces within Japan that are doing their level best to make sure Japan does not change one iota from the sole custody zero sum game, and also to make sure that they will not comply with anything in The Hague. And those people, those individuals, are peppered all throughout the judiciary and the legal system, and so, to shine the light on them is not going to do much, and I am being maybe imprudent by talking about it now. I would like to have said a lot more in my letter to my children, but I have been advised that I have a very, very narrow scope of what I can say, because when it does get over to Japan, it will be spun in such an egregious manner, that even my testimony here today will be cast as some out of control, violent, rageful individual.

Mr. GARRETT. Well, that is not what I have seen.

Mr. Chairman, I thank you for your latitude as it relates to my questioning. And I sincerely ask each of you to reach out to our office with your specifics. And James Van Den Berg is here with me today, and will be working on this subject matter. And, again, I think a realistic goal is that you should receive access to your children. It might even be that you have to travel to them, but, by gosh, that is not a big ask, it is not a big ask. And as a father, again, I can't wrap my brain around what you all have gone through. So——

Ms. HUNTER. Mr. Garrett, may I offer one other piece of information. The Goldman Act certainly does require the State Department to report to you and every Member of Congress, the children who have been abducted and wrongfully retained in another nation. We will certainly get with your office and James to help you identify cases, but you should be receiving this information also from the State Department.

Mr. GARRETT. At the risk of angering the State Department, I find that I receive more forthcoming, good information from private citizens than from the State Department.

Ms. HUNTER. Yes, sir. I agree.

Mr. GARRETT. If anybody from State is here, I apologize.

Thank you, Mr. Chairman.

Mr. SMITH. Thank you, Mr. Garrett.

Let me just conclude with a few final comments. First of all, I want to welcome back Ravi Parmar, who is from my district. He is from Manalapan. His son was abducted to India 4 years ago. He has previously testified, and gave very, very insightful testimony. And, again, like so many others from India, his case remains totally unresolved, and so it is not just disturbing, it needs to be changed, and certainly our hopes are rising that this new administration will do it. The tools are there.

I will give you an example, Dr. Frisancho, your case, Slovakia is trying to, as you know better than anyone else, make you begin your case anew in Hungary because of the proximity of where the children are right next to Slovakia, and yet, the State Department, in the 2016 Goldman report by the State Department, suggested that Slovakia is proof that diplomacy works, and notes in 2015, and I quote,

> U.S. Ambassador to Slovakia joined the chiefs of mission from the French, Irish, Italian, Spanish, and Norwegian Embassies to address problems that parents experienced with the legal system in Slovakia, including a lengthy appeals process and difficulty enforcing Hague Abduction Convention return orders. The Slovak Ministry of Justice introduced new legislation that entered into force on January 1, 2016. The legislation set a twelve-week time limit for the resolution of Convention cases, limits the number of appeals, and provides for expeditious enforcement of Convention orders.

Didn't apply to you. You found no remedy in that. As a matter of fact, ironically, the new limit on appeals is actually preventing you from appealing Slovakia's decision to close your case and to move it to Hungary.

For its part, the U.S. Government is refusing to get involved in "legal matters." That is an abandonment of you, frankly, and I apologize for the State Department for doing that. Yes, there are some very good Foreign Service Officers that take these cases seriously, work hard on them, and I applaud them and have singled them out over and over again. But time and time again, without an MOU, without vigorous enforcement of Hague where Hague is in force, and without the penalty phase prescribed in the Goldman Act, these countries like we saw with the Foreign Minister of Japan, they go to their Parliament and say, the Americans don't enforce their own law. There have been no sanctions meted out to any nation under the Obama administration, and that has got to change with this administration. Doctor, you might want to speak to that, if you would like, but it seems a twisted way of applauding a country, and yet, you have been so further penalized by even a law that we lift up as being a good one.

Dr. FRISANCHO. Yes, Chairman Smith. The truth is that my wife and her parents, they live on the border between Slovakia and Hungary.

Mr. SMITH. Right.

Dr. FRISANCHO. It is only 14 miles distance from the house in Slovakia to the school that the children attend in Hungary. She holds two jobs. She works in Slovakia and in Hungary. It is like keeping one foot in each country. I think she is hoping that we are going to transfer the whole litigation to Hungary, and once Hungarian judges decide that this is wrong again and the children have to return back to the United States, I think she believes she can go again to Slovakia. And it is just this game, like ping-pong.

I have explained all this to the State Department years ago, and I have met with a couple of officials from there, and they have told me, they have advised me that it would be good to start a new case in Hungary. And I have repeatedly said that I don't think this is the best idea, because how can we start a new litigation in Hungary when Slovakia has accumulated evidence for 6 years. That just doesn't make sense.

I also would like to note that one of my Slovakian lawyers advised me and said, Dr. Frisancho, I am a Slovakian citizen and I know how our people think. If Slovakian authorities are getting these demarches, diplomatic notes, and whatever from the U.S. Embassy, that is not going to work. You have to ask the State Department to directly contact the Minister of Justice or someone in Slovakia at the highest level.

I have repeatedly said that to the State Department for years, and my case managers have always answered, we have to escalate, but we are escalating for years, and we never got to the top. As I said before, I am very grateful for what they have done for me and for my children, but we all can see that nothing of this works. So if I could ask one more thing from the State Department, it would be to follow the instructions of a Slovakian lawyer that is a Slovakian citizen. He knows what he is saying. He understands the Slovakian mentality.

They are not going to listen to these diplomatic notes, personal meetings, demarches. They are upset, of course, that Slovakia has appeared on the report of noncompliance. They are upset, I am sure, that they lost a case under the European Court of Human Rights.

They had to pay me damages, with that they had to acknowledge that they did wrong, they violated my human rights, but the cases are still pending, and it is because we need more pressure from the top.

Mr. SMITH. I think that point is well spoken, and I thank you for it.

You know, there are others in the audience, Jeffery Morehouse was mentioned; Edeanna Barbirou, who testified some years ago; last year, I believe it was. She has an unenforced order, like so many others. And if there ever was an Achilles heel, there are lots of them, it is the unenforced order. You get the piece of paper, you think, I got it, and then it is not enforced. This is the first hearing this year on child abduction. It will be followed by several others, including inviting the Trump administration to send its top representatives here, and I hope the same thing happens on the Senate side, to begin an all-out effort to enforce the law, the U.S. law, and find if there needs to be any additions to it, but above all, enforce what we have got. It was painstakingly arrived at. I introduced it 5 years before it was actually enacted and went over it multiple times, always looking to finely tune it. The Senate wouldn't take it up, and then they finally did, thank God, and we were able to get it down to the President for signature. A law that is unenforced is just sitting on the table. We need enforcement, and that is going to be my mantra going forward, I can assure you.

Anything you would like to add before we conclude? And I thank you again for coming forward. And I certainly, as a father myself, so deeply respect your love for your children, and all of us feel that way on my staff, that we are just in awe of your tenacity, of your love. And so if there is anything you would like to say, or we will just conclude.

Yes, Doctor.

Dr. FRISANCHO. I would like just to send a short message to all the fathers and mothers who are dealing with similar cases.

What the abductor wants, and sometimes the courts in their countries, and all the authorities in their countries who are supporting the abductors, what they want is to wear you out. Please stay strong. Find any kind of support in your church, your friends. You see how many people I got here today. You have to fight for your children. And use us as an example. Look at Noelle, James, everybody here, Edeanna, Randy, and so many people.

We struggle. We cannot sleep. We think of our children all the time. And we know what this means for you, so please, you have to keep going, stay strong and fight. Your children will appreciate it one day. And you have to make sure that they know. Like my kids, I don't think they know. The National Center for Missing and Exploited Children just helped me to publish my blog in December 2010.

For the first time, my kids have the opportunity to see something about me. When I went to courts, I almost never spoke anything wrong about my wife. The court proceedings took place mainly about her accusing me of everything possible, and me and my lawyers defending. But I changed my mind, and so from this year, I am going to start making all the real information public so that my children can see that. And I cannot just live without continuing trying to help my children. It is nothing against the mother. I believe that there is a law, and we have to fight to make sure that those who are responsible have to fulfill the law. So parents, please, stay strong and keep fighting for your children.

That is all what I wanted to say. Thank you.

Mr. SMITH. Thank you.

Ms. HUNTER. Mr. Chairman, thank you. Just in closing, a few words from us.

We truly do believe, again, that this is the time to put America first for America's stolen children. We expect this administration to hold true to that as it relates to this vulnerable population.

Transparency is very, very important. Good data from the State Department reported to Congress, you can use, and we as an organizing and growing parent community can use. We are not going away. More parents are coming along every day that believe that there is a solution and the only solution is children returning home. And then we call for strong leadership in the Office of Children's Issues that would make this a transformative process. Thank you.

Mr. SMITH. Thank you so very much.

[Whereupon, at 1:54 p.m., the subcommittee was adjourned.]

A P P E N D I X

Material Submitted for the Record

SUBCOMMITTEE HEARING NOTICE
COMMITTEE ON FOREIGN AFFAIRS
U.S. HOUSE OF REPRESENTATIVES
WASHINGTON, DC 20515-6128

Subcommittee on Africa, Global Health, Global Human Rights, and International Organizations
Christopher H. Smith (R-NJ), Chairman

April 6, 2017

TO: **MEMBERS OF THE COMMITTEE ON FOREIGN AFFAIRS**

You are respectfully requested to attend an OPEN hearing of the Committee on Foreign Affairs, to be held by the Subcommittee on Africa, Global Health, Global Human Rights, and International Organizations in Room 2172 of the Rayburn House Office Building (and available live on the Committee website at http://www.ForeignAffairs.house.gov):

DATE: Thursday, April 6, 2017

TIME: 12:00 p.m.

SUBJECT: Enforcement is Not Optional: The Goldman Act to Return Abducted American Children

WITNESSES: Noelle Hunter, Ph.D.
Co-founder
iStand Parent Network
(Mother of Child Returned from Mali)

Mr. James Cook
(Father of Children Abducted to Japan)

Augusto Frisancho, M.D.
(Father of Children Abducted to Slovakia)

Mr. Vikram Jagtiani
Co-founder
Bring Our Kids Home
(Father of Child Abducted to India)

By Direction of the Chairman

The Committee on Foreign Affairs seeks to make its facilities accessible to persons with disabilities. If you are in need of special accommodations, please call 202/225-5021 at least four business days in advance of the event, whenever practicable. Questions with regard to special accommodations in general (including availability of Committee materials in alternative formats and assistive listening devices) may be directed to the Committee.

COMMITTEE ON FOREIGN AFFAIRS

MINUTES OF SUBCOMMITTEE ON _Africa, Global Health, Global Human Rights, and International Organizations_ HEARING

Day_ _Thursday_ _Date_ _April 6, 2017_ _Room _2172 Rayburn HOB_

Starting Time _12:03 p.m._ Ending Time _1:54 p.m._

Recesses [_0_] (___to___) (___to___) (___to___) (___to___) (___to___) (___to___)

Presiding Member(s)

Rep. Chris Smith

Check all of the following that apply:

Open Session ☑
Executive (closed) Session ☐
Televised ☑

Electronically Recorded (taped) ☑
Stenographic Record ☑

TITLE OF HEARING:

Enforcement is Not Optional: The Goldman Act to Return Abducted American Children

SUBCOMMITTEE MEMBERS PRESENT:

Rep. Tom Garrett

NON-SUBCOMMITTEE MEMBERS PRESENT: _(Mark with an * if they are not members of full committee.)_

HEARING WITNESSES: Same as meeting notice attached? Yes ☑ No ☐
(If "no", please list below and include title, agency, department, or organization.)

STATEMENTS FOR THE RECORD: _(List any statements submitted for the record.)_

Statement of Mr. Charles Ferrao, submitted by Rep. Chris Smith

TIME SCHEDULED TO RECONVENE _____
or
TIME ADJOURNED _1:54 p.m._

Subcommittee Staff Associate

Material submitted for the record by the Honorable Christopher H. Smith, a Representative in Congress from the State of New Jersey, and chairman, Subcommittee on Africa, Global Health, Global Human Rights, and International Organizations

STATEMENT OF CHARLES FERRAO ON THE THE KIDNAPPING OF HELENA AND HENRIQUE DE NOGUEIRA FERRAO TO UGANDA (AFRICA)

Honorable members of this subcommittee. I am Helena and Henrique´s father, my children were kidnapped on January 24, 2015 by their mother, Colette Okanya (aka Sheila Komuntale, Colette Kanyunuzi etc.) with the full support of her mother, Evelyn Komuntale (aka Georgette Gerard) of OutreachtoAfrica.org under the false pretenses of a five week vacation.

When Colette did not return home with our children on her due date of March 8, 2015, I purchased an extra set of tickets for her to return on March 12, 2015 while garnering her assurances she would return on that date. She never did.

As with most parents of kidnapped children, I immediately turned for help from the Long Beach Police Department and the Los Angeles County District Attorney's Child Abduction Unit only to find out the nightmare of first having to go through Family Court in order to secure full legal, sole and physical rights to the children.

By August 5, 2015, two family court judges and countless hearings I gained full custody of my children and by August 25, the Prosecutor charged Colette with two felony counts for abducting our children. It should be noted that the judges, police detective and the prosecutor, each afforded Colette the opportunity to return with the children, or send them home without any consequences to her criminal and selfish actions. Yet she took advantage of some seven chances given to her and to date remains defiant in kidnapping our children and completely alienating them from me, and my family. Needless to say the suffering cannot be expressed on paper for words alone would not do it justice.

It should be noted that the last time the children and I had any contact, was via Skype, on August 1, 2015; in that communication, my then, brave four year old, little girl said "Daddy, I'm not okay, I love you, I miss you, I wanna come home," my then three year old little boy jumped in and said that he too missed and loved me and wanted to come home. Those were their last pleas of desperation, to me, where I was left helpless to secure their return home.

I was then told by the Prosecutor's office that they would make no efforts to seek out and rescue my children, since Uganda was not a signatory of the Hague treaty, whereby nations would collaborate with their respective government entities to return kidnapped children to their home countries.

I refused to accept this, and took it upon myself to embark on a mission to bring Helena and Henrique home. I'd had over two decades of law enforcement and criminal justice experience under my belt, and applied that and other learned skills for this endeavor.

After squaring away with the State Department and Interpol, I turned my attention to any possible family members of the kidnappers, who might not agree with such a heinous crime and selfish actions against innocent children. Thankfully, there were some cousins of theirs that in fact found the kidnapping deplorable and many times indicated that the children belonged with me here in the U.S. and could not understand why Colette would deprive them of a better life, especially since she, had enjoyed the American dream for half of her own life.

After establishing these contacts, one of the cousins volunteered to bring me the children. This offer was presented to Colette and should that been accepted by her, I had assured her family, that if she returned later, that so long as she took a plea offer from the prosecutor, she would avoid jail and also would share the children with her equally and even furnish her with voluntary, half child support. As you might imagine, she scoffed at the offer and remained defiant.

I was finally given contact to some mid-level, ranking Uganda police personnel, and upon establishing a relationship, was able to convince them to start a rescue mission of the children and expressed to them that I was no interested in the kidnappers but the sole return of Helena and Henri. I was told by the team leader that the police commissioner was happy to see that I was not out to seek revenge (i.e. have Colette extradited to the U.S. to have her go to prison) but merely wanting my children back.

The Ugandan police then initiated contact with our Prosecutor requesting the arrest warrant, Interpol notices and within a matter of weeks, the team found Colette hiding with our children, her mother and presumably Colette's new man in a Kampala Hotel. She was arrested, the mother detained and the children taken into protective custody. It was noted that the U.S. Embassy had been closed by quarter of an hour and the children would remain in the care of the police overnight.

The following events are the very basis of my appeal to the subcommittee and why the enforcement of the Goldman Act are critical.

Within a few short hours of Colette's arrest, her mother contacted Uganda's Assistant Inspector General of the Police, and Director of Interpol Asan Kasyngie and Colette was immediately released (and without cause) while I impress she remains a wanted criminal fugitive by Interpol on a red notice (the world's most powerful type of arrest warrant) while the children remain on Interpol, yellow notices (for their kidnapping status). Needless to say, myself and many in the law enforcement community here, were left in disbelief that Uganda's Interpol Chief, who admitted had had previous, sit down meetings with a criminal fugitive (as acknowledged to their premiere newspaper, The Vision) wanted by the very agency he was in charge of and refused to uphold the laws governing Interpol, but more dismally permitting a Congolese criminal fugitive in his country to kidnap two American children.

Fast forwarding from this event, the U.S. State Department sent two diplomatic notices to Uganda's Minister of Foreign Affairs and top law enforcement officer, the Inspector General of Police, only to be substantively ignored by them. This clearly demonstrates that the Ugandan government (a nation that receives millions in U.S. tax dollars regularly, along with military hardware such as combat helicopters, so the regime can subjugate its citizens) is perfectly willing to protect foreigners (in this case Congolese nationals) wanted by U.S. Authorities and Interpol. Even worse, Uganda demonstrates that it is willing to aid and abet in the ongoing kidnapping of two, innocent American children.

It should be noted that the grandmother owns a non-profit (OutreachtoAfrica, a 501©3 registered in California) purportedly to save orphans in Africa, but it is known she has been paying many officials in Uganda thousands of dollars in bribes to allow her and her criminal fugitive daughter to move about the country without a care in the world due to the protection these two women receive from this rogue nation.

I then joined I-Stand (a US non-profit, intended to help families of parentally kidnapped children) in our nation's capital last April, where I had the opportunity to meet with our elected officials and even had two personal meetings with the ambassadors of Uganda and Portugal (European Union). The ambassador of Portugal, with Portugal's faithful allegiance to the U.S., promptly wrote a diplomatic letter to the ambassador of Uganda to return my American children home to me. Senator Feinstein and Congressman Lowenthal did the same.

Then in June of 2016, a cousin of the fugitives desperately reached out to me citing Helena had sustained a bad beating (though refusing to tell me who the perpetrator was) and furnished me a photo of my child, with a black eye, bruises and in a guarded nearly fetal positions (all indicative of an abused child) urging me to have the U.S. Embassy send out a rescue team. I can only tell you that I was in my office when I received the photo, fell out of my chair and cried for some twenty minutes until I regained my composure and immediately reached out to all of the respective, involved agencies and begged for help, now knowing one of my children had been abused.

Ultimately, I reached out to Congressman Smith of NJ, who agreed to go a step further by requesting that the Foreign Ministry investigate our complaint and take all necessary action to redress this situation. Mr. Smith is the author of the Goldman Act, and speaks on behalf of thousands of parents whose children were kidnapped overseas and who are desperately hoping for the actual enforcement of this noble law to ensure that once and for all, our nation's abducted children overseas are returned to their loving family homes, where they belong.

I know I speak for hundreds of parents who face my predicament in seeking the safe return of our beloved, innocent abducted to countries that receive U.S. aid, yet refuse to return our American children.

As such, I appeal to this honorable subcommittee to please use the Goldman Act in full force and return my beloved Helena and Henri home. With Helena having been abused, I fear constantly for her safety and that of Henri as well. Lord knows I have shed rivers of tears for my children as has my mother, who buried a son and now fears she will never see her grandchildren again. Please help me and the countless other parents who too suffer in the loss of their kidnapped American children. Thank you.

www.ingramcontent.com/pod-product-compliance
Lightning Source LLC
Chambersburg PA
CBHW081236280526
45787CB00006B/2681